THE GOLD GUIDES

FLORENCE

*New Florence guide updated to January 2002
with accurate descriptions of all the major artworks.
All the typical dishes of Florentine cuisine.*

BB
BONECHI

CONTENTS

Publication created and designed by Casa Editrice Bonechi.
Publication manager: Serena de Leonardis.
Picture research,Graphic design: Serena de Leonardis. Make-up: Federica Balloni.
Cover: Laura Settesoldi. Editing: Anna Baldini.
Cartography: Carla Zucchi, Centro Studi Tecnici, Sesto Fiorentino (Firenze).

Text by Patrizia Fabbri, Stefano Masi and by the editorial staff of the publisher
Text for "Lunchtime" (pages 173-189): Paolo Piazzesi
Translations: Anthony Brierley (pages 11-168); Paula Boomsliter (Introductions and "Lunchtime")

Printed in Italy by Centro Stampa Editoriale Bonechi - Sesto Fiorentino

Photographs from the Archives of Casa Editrice Bonechi taken by Gaetano Barone, Marco
Bonechi, Carlo Cantini, Serena de Leonardis, Andrea Fantauzzo, Paolo Giambone, Dario
Grimoldi, Italfotogieffe, M.S.A., Andrea Pistolesi, Antonio Quattrone

Page 45 below, courtesy of Cassa di Risparmio di Firenze

ISBN 88-476-0980-1

* * *

*F*rom the Roman military encampment established by Julius Caesar in 59 BC on the right bank of the Arno arose the Roman Florentia, with its uniform, squared-off lines today hidden in the substrates of the historical center, and then the medieval city that survived the barbarian invasions, cut through by alleyways and punctuated by soaring stone towers, symbols of prestige for the ancient, powerful families. From the 12th to the 13th century the craft guilds or corporazioni, especially that of the merchants, grew in power together with the wealth of the city, which became an internationally-important economic center. The period spanning the 13th and 16th centuries was the time of that revolution which, thanks to patronage of the great and wealthy Florentine families (with the Medici at the top of the list), transformed it into the grandiose "city of art" known to all the world: that 16th-century Florence at the height of its urbanistic and monumental splendor, that city depicted in its entirety by Vasari in his celebrated Siege of Florence (1530). But the city, shown from a vantage point above San Miniato, was then still lacking one of its major architectural masterpieces, by that same Vasari: the Uffizi and the passage known as the Vasari Corridor, completed in 1580.

Over the centuries, the structure of the city has kept faith with the plan that saw its birth and its natural development along the course of the Arno, harmoniously surrounded by the green hills from which urban development shied but nevertheless placed a few yet excellent constructions.

TIMELINE

HISTORICAL

8th - 1st century B.C.

Already occupied in prehistoric times, an Etruscan settlement is formed as early as the 8th century B. C. to control the ford across the Arno where the Ponte Vecchio now stands. In 59 B.C. the Roman colony of **Florentia** is founded.

1st - 10th century

The spread of Christianity begins in the 4th century and the first churches are built. With the fall of the Empire come the invasions of the Ostrogoths (405), Byzantines (539), Goths (541) and Longobards (570). In the Carolingian period (8th century) a feudal system is established and Florence becomes a territory of the Holy Roman Empire.

11th - 12th century

Having become a commune, Florence clashes with neighbouring communes such as Fiesole, which is besieged and partially destroyed.

8th - 1st century B.C.

The **Forum**, the **Capitolium**, **baths**, a **theatre**, an **amphitheatre** and **walls** are to be found around the two main streets of the Roman colony (Via Roma - Via Calimala and Via Strozzi - Via del Corso). The town, although small and self-contained, is founded as an intermediate stopping point controlling important trade routes between north and south and between coast and hinterland that had already existed in pre-Etruscan times.

1st - 10th century

Although many buildings were erected in the Roman period (now buried and identified in recent archaeologial excavations), with the fall of the Empire, the city, a trading centre, declines, and under the Byzantines decreases in size. In the Carolingian period there is a revival with increased economic activity. After the **first churches** have been built (San Lorenzo), the circuit of city walls is enlarged and suburbs spring up outside the main gates.

11th - 12th century

The circuit of the walls is extended to include the left bank of the river and the **Baptistery** and **San Miniato al Monte** are built.The consolidation of communal life leads to a more active economy and a resulting increase in population.

8th - 1st century B.C.

Etruscan civilization did not leave us remains of any particular artistic importance in the urban Florence area. In nearby communities, however, we find the tombs of Sesto Fiorentino, the temple and walls of Fiesole, and the funerary stelae near Pontassieve. The cultural development of the area fits a facies typical of northern Etruscan Tuscany.

1st - 10th century

The cultural and artistic life of the Roman city dies out as a result of the invasions and continues only in the field of religion. From the 8th century culture starts to revive thanks to the Carolingian schools.

11th - 12th century

Romanesque art establishes itself. In Florence it is characterized by the external facing of religious buildings in polychrome marble. Sculpture, as well as being used in architecture, becomes a work of art in its own right. Painting instead remains tied to the Byzantine tradition.

13th century

The commune of Florence becomes more important, despite the struggles between Guelfs (supporters of the pope) and Ghibellines (supporters of the German Emperors). The emergence of the "popolo grasso", backed by the Guelfs, leads to a policy of open clashes for supremacy with neighbouring Tuscan communes. The aristocratic classes see their power diminish as economic development leads to the rise of classes of entrepreneurs, merchants and bankers, who form the Arti Maggiori (Major Guilds). From the middle of the century communal power rests in their hands. There is a considerable increase in population.

13th century

The city consists of **tower-houses** which are easy to defend in case of attack by other Florentine factions. The network of city streets becomes particulary intricate. **Palazzo Vecchio** and the **Duomo** are built in the new Gothic style, together with the **Bargello.**

13th century

The Gothic style, which originated in France, spreads, although the original lightness of the style, characterized by a soaring vertical thrust, is heavier here. Examples in Florence are Santa Maria Novella and Santa Croce. Painting in Florence sees the emergence of two great figures, Cimabue and Giotto. The former, although still tied to earlier models, is aware of the problems of volume and relief, as can be seen in his *Crucifix* in Santa Croce and the *Maestà* in the Uffizi. Giotto, in his work, succeeds in conveying a sense of three-dimensionality, realism of expression and environmental setting.

14th century

The domination of the middle classes is threatened by the serious crisis arising from the failure of the kings of Naples and England to pay back large debts. Following the tyranny of the Duke of Athens in the middle of the century and the plague of 1348, there are various revolts by the lower classes. The middle classes, now establishing themselves in power, begin to oppress the lower classes, who rebel with Ciuto Brandini and then with the Ciompi Revolt, succeeding in driving

14th century

The **Ponte Vecchio,** part of the **Duomo, Giotto's Campanile, Palazzo Vecchio, Orsanmichele** and the **Loggia del Bigallo** date from this period. In the first half of the century the city is reorganized by the construction of the third, and largest city wall, which also embraces vast areas Oltrarno. Here remains of it can still be seen, while on the right bank only the city gates have survived the 19th-century clearance and rebuilding.

14th century

In sculpture great artists are at work: Arnolfo di Cambio, who designed the facade of the Duomo that was later destroyed, as well as outsiders such as Tino di Camaino, Andrea and Nino Pisano. The figure of Giotto influences the entire peninsula and in the city generates a school that includes Taddeo Gaddi, Maso di Banco and Bernardo Daddi. In the middle of the century Andrea Orcagna and Nardo di Cione come to the fore, together with many other artists whose

out the Priors and forming three new Guilds which participate briefly in the government of the city.

works even today enrich the city's churches. In the field of literature there are Dante, Boccaccio and Petrarch. The "stil novo" and the Divine Comedy make the vernacular a language to be reckoned with on a national level, coloured by Florentine characteristics that will be taken up everywhere..

15th century

The wealthy classes once again dominate. The most influential Florentine families - Pitti, Capponi, Alberti, Uzzano, Albizi and Medici - struggle for supremacy. In 1433 the Medicis prevail with Cosimo il Vecchio: his grandson Lorenzo will become the key figure in European politics and culture of the time. Later, Piero de' Medici will succumb to Charles VIII. The city continues to flourish economically throughout the century, though in the final years of the 15th century the popular need for democracy and religious reform comes to a head in the figure of Girolamo Savonarola.

15th century

Numerous palaces are built for the wealthiest Florentine families (Pitti, Medici) as well as other monuments inspired by the geometric laws of ancient buildings. Brunelleschi designs **Santo Spirito**, **San Lorenzo**, the **Pazzi Chapel** and the **Cupola of the Duomo**.

15th century

The concept of the rationalization of art develops in the cultural circles of this period which is called the 'Renaissance'. The inspiration of classical art and a meticulous study of perspective and the concept of space opens the way for the work of Donatello, Masaccio, Botticelli, Ghiberti, Beato Angelico, Michelozzo, Alberti, Della Robbia, Paolo Uccello, Pollaiolo, Lippi and Brunelleschi.

16th - 17th century

The return to power of the Medici family is consolidated by the election of Giovanni de' Medici to the papacy. The presence in Italy of Charles V of Spain leads to a revolt, followed however by the return to the throne of Alessandro de'Medici. Cosimo creates the regional state. Life in the city gradually loses its initial impulse. Florence stops expanding and the Grand Duchy, from

16th - 17th century

The changes the city undergoes in the 16th century are linked to grand-ducal cultural policy, and after the construction of the **Laurentian Library** and the **New Sacristy** by Michelangelo, the city is enriched by the **Uffizi**, the **Logge del Pesce**, the **Boboli Gardens**, the **Logge of the Mercato Nuovo** and the **Ponte di Santa Trinita**, as well as numerous private palaces. Mannerist

16th - 17th century

Early Renaissance forms become too limiting for 16th-century artists, since what they now want to express is man's new desire to dominate nature, as in the works of Leonardo da Vinci, Michelangelo, Raphael and Andrea del Sarto, until new living conditions will lead to the sensibilities of Mannerism. From this, through the works of the Carracci and Caravaggio, the next step is the Baroque.

being a commercial power becomes primarily agricultural.

buildings, some displaying peculiar flights of fancy, appear between the 16th and 17th century. On the whole, however, urban building activity slows up in the 17th century and is generally limited to a retouching or renovation of extant works.

Artists of this period are Cellini, Vasari and Giambologna, and in literature, Machiavelli. The Accademia della Crusca and the Accademia del Cimento are founded.

18th - 19th - 20th century

In the 18th century the Grand Duchy is ruled by the Hapsburg-Lorraine dynasty, and thanks to various reforms introduced by Pietro Leopoldo the economy revives. After the period of French domination between the 18th and 19th century the Lorraine family reclaims the Chiana and the Maremma. Despite overtures to the liberals, a triumvirate is constituted for the concession of the Constitution. The abolition of the corporations, which date back to the Middle Ages, and the relaunching of small farm-holdings by the Lorraine are followed by pressure from the liberals who, having obtained the statute, freedom of the press and the presence of the civil guard (1847), now intend to obtain the constitution from the Grand Duke, to the point that he is expelled. Grand-duke leopold, having fled the city, returns with the support of the Austrians, but in 1859 is finally forced to abandon it. Annexed to Piedmont in 1859, Florence becomes capital of Italy. The history of the city follows the historical fortunes of the country through the two World Wars.

18th - 19th - 20th century

As regards town planning, in the 18th century unhealthy dwellings for the poor take over the centre, while the middle classes build up their own distinctive residential districts. The construction of two railway stations is followed by a rebuilding of the centre and the demolition of the walls to reclaim slums and make the city more prestigious (project by Poggi). As the capital city, the rapidity of the industrial and demographic development of the city leads to damage with inevitable consequences up to the present day (allotting of habitable and green areas, traffic, economic initiatives). In the 20th century the new railway **station of Santa Maria Novella** is built by Giovanni Michelucci, followed by the destruction during the War of the bridges over the Arno (only Ponte Vecchio escapes destruction).

18th - 19th - 20th century

In the 19th century the dictates of the Accademia di Belle Arti, linked to the political policies, influence the sculpture of Dupré and Bartolini. Quite different are the works of Cecioni, linked to the fresh spontaneity of the Macchiaioli painters. The latter, dedicated to a break with the academism of the Ussi and the Benvenuti, use spots of color to depict subjects of everyday life that are usually neglected. Besides Fattori, mention must be made of Signorini, Costa and Lega. In the 20th century Rosai and Corti work in Florence. In the broader field of culture, the presence of the group of Futurists must be noted. Art in the city is seriously damaged by the flood of November 4, 1966, which destroys or damages numerous works.

INDEX OF WALKING TOURS

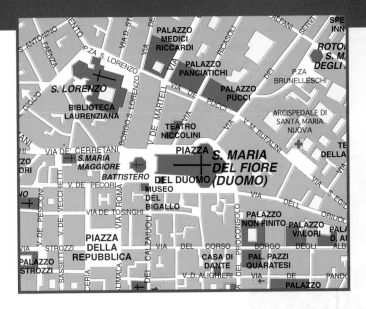

Piazza del Duomo and San Lorenzo

*P*iazza del Duomo, in the suggestive cornice of the green, pink, and white marbles of its three major buildings, embraces the religious heart of the city. It all begins with the geometrical, luminous elegance of the Baptistry of San Giovanni, which according to medieval tradition was built over a Roman-age temple of Mars; it continues with the dazzling Duomo, built over the early Christian church of Santa Reparata, and with Giotto's famous freestanding Campanile. All around are the ancient headquarters' of historical public assistance organizations, like the Compag-

nia del Bigallo that owned the beautiful loggia on Piazza San Giovanni. Another extraordinary sight is the panorama of the city from the top of Brunelleschi's dome (but, unfortunately, there are no elevators); even if you decide to skip the climb, be sure to visit the Museo dell'Opera del Duomo, which preserves works from the Baptistry, the Campanile, and the Duomo, including a number of true masterpieces. Leaving Piazza del Duomo behind, we penetrate the "Medici" territory of Palazzo Medici Riccardi and the adjacent Piazza San Lorenzo. Here, a few steps away from the stands of the crowded open-air market, the Cappelle Medicee bring together some of the greatest works left us by Michelangelo.

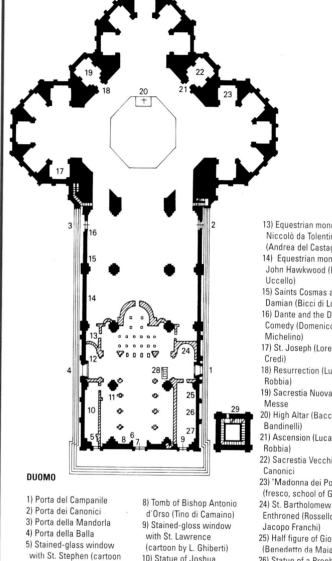

DUOMO

1) Porta del Campanile
2) Porta dei Canonici
3) Porta della Mandorla
4) Porta della Balla
5) Stained-glass window with St. Stephen (cartoon by L. Ghiberti)
6) Stained-glass window with the Assumption (cartoon by L. Ghiberti)
7) Coronation of the Virgin (Gaddo Gaddi)
8) Tomb of Bishop Antonio d'Orso (Tino di Camaino)
9) Stained-gloss window with St. Lawrence (cartoon by L. Ghiberti)
10) Statue of Joshua (Ciuffagni, Donatello, Nanni di Bartolo)
11) Edicule of St. Zanobius (Giovanni del Biondo)
12) Bust of A. Squarcialupi (Benedetto da Maiano)
13) Equestrian monument to Niccolò da Tolentino (Andrea del Castagno)
14) Equestrian monument to John Hawkwood (Paolo Uccello)
15) Saints Cosmas and Damian (Bicci di Lorenzo)
16) Dante and the Divine Comedy (Domenico di Michelino)
17) St. Joseph (Lorenzo di Credi)
18) Resurrection (Luca della Robbia)
19) Sacrestia Nuova or delle Messe
20) High Altar (Baccio Bandinelli)
21) Ascension (Luca della Robbia)
22) Sacrestia Vecchia or dei Canonici
23) "Madonna dei Popolo" (fresco, school of Giotto)
24) St. Bartholomew Enthroned (Rossello di Jacopo Franchi)
25) Half figure of Giotto (Benedetto da Maiano
26) Statue of a Prophet (Nanni di Banco)
27) Bust of Brunelleschi (Buggiano)
28) Entrance to the Crypt of Santa Reparata
29) Giotto's Campanile

DUOMO or CATHEDRAL OF SANTA MARIA DEL FIORE

On 8 September 1296 Cardinal Pietro Valeriano laid the first stone of Florence cathedral, a building constructed in several stages in the course of numerous centuries and, so to speak, "completed" in 1887 with the construction of the present facade. The task of building the cathedral was initially entrusted to Arnolfo di Cambio, who worked on it until his death in 1302. It was built on the site of the old **church of Santa Reparata** and this name continued to be used for the cathedral up until the 15th century, when it was changed to Santa Maria del Fiore. Arnolfo supervised the construction of part of the facade and built the outer walls around those of Santa Reparata, which continued to be used as a church until 1375. Following Arnolfo's death the building of the cathedral proceeded in fits and starts. In 1331 work resumed with greater speed thanks to the magistrates of the Wool Guild who founded the OPA, the 'Opera del Duomo', an institution whose purpose was to supervise the construction of the building. In 1334 Giotto was appointed chief architect of the Opera. He devoted almost all his energies to the building of the campanile (bell-tower) until his death in 1337. Following a period of inactivity lasting about twenty years, Francesco Talenti and

A view of the facade of the Duomo.

Giovanni di Lapo Ghini were appointed to the supervise building work. Although they modified Arnolfo's original design, they continued the work of their predecessors. In 1367 a competition was held to decide on the definitive design of the cathedral. Of all the models presented the one chosen was the work of four architects and four painters, including Andrea Orcagna, Taddeo Gaddi and Andrea di Bonaiuto, who portrayed their design for the cathedral in the *Allegory of the Church* frescoed in Santa Maria Novella.

Between 1378 and 1421, following the demolition of the church of Santa Reparata which by this time was hindering the continuation of work, the building of the new cathedral proceeded steadily. After the completion of the vaults of the nave and side aisles the tribunes were built, as was the drum of the **cupola**, which had been foreseen in Arnolfo's original design. Because the construction of the cupola posed considerable technical problems, in 1418 another competition was held to decide on the model. Amid great controversy the Opera chose the design presented by Filippo Brunelleschi, who finished building the cupola in 1436. On 25 March of the same year Pope Eugenius IV consecrated the cathedral, which was named Santa Maria del Fiore.

Nevertheless, the great building was still far from being finished. In 1471 the **lantern** crowning the cupola was completed, although work continued throughout the 15th and 16th centuries on both the arrangement of the interior and the external marble decoration, which, in addition to the sides and absidal area extended also to the drum of the cupola, along one side of which Baccio d'Agnolo built a gallery. Further additions and modifications were made right up until the end of the 19th century, when the **facade** was built.

Crypt of Santa Reparata - In 1966, during a series of archeological excavations inside the Duomo, the remains of the ancient metropolitan church dedicated to Santa Reparata, who was martyred in Caesarea, were brought to light. The church occupied the site where the great cathedral of Santa Maria del Fiore now stands. The walls of the present cathedral were in fact erected around the earlier building, which continued to be used as a place of worship until 1375, when the ancient structure was demolished so that the vaults of the nave and aisles could be closed and the roof of the new church built.

The church of Santa Reparata was built between the 4th and 5th century over the foundations of a house of Roman Florence. Destroyed by the troops of Totila during the Gothic invasions, the church was later completely rebuilt. The original basilical form with a nave and two side aisles was preserved, though it was enlarged by the building of various chapels in the area of the transept. Around the year 1000 a crypt was added and two bell-towers were built at the sides of the apse. Among the various attractions of the crypt are some fine mosaic pavements dating from the oldest phase of the building's history, various frescoes and numerous tomb slabs of important figures, both secular and religious, of medieval Florence, including that of Filippo Brunelleschi, whose tomb was brought to light in 1972.

The dome of the Duomo and tombstones in the Crypt of Santa Reparata.

Facade - The original design for the facade was conceived by Arnolfo di Cambio, who was responsible not only for its architectural composition but also for various statues that were made as decorative elements. The iconographical programme of the Arnolfian facade, only the lower third of which was built, was a celebration of the Virgin and the city of Florence through its most venerated and emblematic figures.

In the lunette of the central door was a statue of the Madonna and Child, flanked by statues of Santa Reparata and St Zenobius, and surmounted by two Angels. The decoration of the facade with statues continued in the 14th and 15th centuries. Eminent artists such as Nanni di Banco and Donatello worked on it, the latter producing an intensely expressive statue of St John. The sculptures were intended to stand out vividly against the white, green and pink polychrome marble facing of the facade.

Already during the Renaissance plans were made to replace the 14th-century facade with a new one more in keeping with contemporary tastes, although this happened only in 1587, when the original Arnolfian facade was demolished on the orders of Grand-duke Francesco I de' Medici by the architect Bernardo Buontalenti. After the demolition of the original facade the front of the cathe-

dral was decorated with temporary coverings and finally frescoed with an elaborate architectural painting by Ercole Graziani for the wedding of Prince Ferdinando de' Medici with Violante of Bavaria in 1688. The present facade was designed by the architect Emilio De Fabris, whose basilical model prevailed over various tricuspidal models (such as Santa Croce) in two separate competitions held in the second half of the 19th century. Work began in 1871 and was completed in 1887 and followed a decorative programme inspired by the original Arnolfian design, devoted to the glorification of the Madonna and the celebration of Christianity. The *Virgin and Child* by Tito Sarrocchi occupies the central niche of the **Gallery of Apostles**, which runs all the way across the facade. Particular emphasis was also given to the history of the cathedral with the statues of *Cardinal Valeriani, Bishop Tinacci* and *Sant'Antonino*, who blessed, respectively, the first stone, the first pilaster and the lantern, and *Pope Eugenius IV*, who consecrated the cathedral in 1436.

Cupola - The plan to cover the octagonal space formed by the crossing of the nave and transept with a cupola took shape in the

second half of the 14th century. The original idea, for which Francesco Talenti was partly responsible, did not envisage the high drum we see today, but rather a covering grafted onto the body of the cathedral immediately above the half-domes of the tribunes, as we can see from the reproduction of the cathedral painted by Andrea di Bonaiuto in his *Allegory of the Church*. In 1418, following numerous changes of plan during the various building phases, a competition was held to decide on the cupola's definitive design. Amid much controversy the model presented by Filippo Brunelleschi prevailed and work on the cupola started two years later. Brunelleschi's design was a revolutionary departure from conventional systems of construction since it dispensed with the need for a supporting timber centering during the building phase. The alternative proposed by Brunelleschi was a self-supporting structure consisting of two domes, with a space between them, resting on a high octagonal drum. The inner shell, measuring more than two metres thick, was

Filippo BRUNELLESCHI
(1377-1446)

Florentine sculptor and goldsmith, but above all the unrivalled master of an architecture imbued with a new classicism and a successful application of the laws of perspective. Brunelleschi travelled widely and carried out meticulous technical studies in Rome before engaging in that prodigious activity which between 1419 and 1446 blossomed in Florence in a whole series of splendid masterpieces: the Spedale degli Innocenti, San Lorenzo, the Pazzi Chapel, the Palagio di Parte Guelfa, Santo Spirito and the cupola of Santa Maria del Fiore, the cathedral where he had the honour, as the only layman, of being buried.

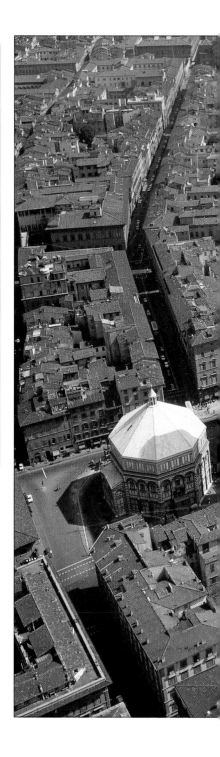

made of bricks laid in a 'herring-bone' pattern and arranged in such a way as to form pointed vaults that tapered up to the base of the lantern. The outer shell, made from red terracotta tiles, functioned as a roof covering. It was linked to the inner shell by vertical stone ribs, the ones at the corners where the 8 segments were joined together being 'visible', in a certain sense, since they were covered by the 9 external marble ribs. The space between the two shells was used for stairs that led up to the top of the cupola crowned by the lantern. The lantern was completed many years after Brunelleschi's death in 1446, ten years after the inauguration of his masterpiece in 1436. Even after the construction of the lantern, the cupola was not considered properly finished. As the detail of the cathedral reproduced by Domenico di Michelino in the painting *Dante explaining the Divine Comedy* (1465) shows, the marble facing of the drum was still missing. To complete the decoration of the drum it was decided to build a gallery. This was begun by Baccio d'Agnolo in 1506 but interrupted after about a decade following criticism of Michelangelo, who dubbed it a "crickets' cage".

The **Lantern** was envisaged in the original project drawn up by Brunelleschi, which won the competition of 1418, though its formal and architectural details had not been defined. When work on the cupola had been completed, therefore, another competition was held which was again won by Filippo Brunelleschi. He worked on the construction of the lantern for a decade, from 1436 to 1446, though he never saw it built in his own lifetime. Its construction was the work of other eminent architects, primarily Michelozzo and Verrocchio. The latter, in fact, was responsible for the completion of the lantern, for which, between 1468 and 1471, he made the gilded bronze *ball* that was placed at the top. In 1601 the ball was destroyed by a bolt of lightning and later rebuilt.

The interior of the Duomo.

PAOLO UCCELLO
**Equestrian monument
to John Hawkwood**
(1436)

This unusual fresco in chiaroscuro *portrays the English soldier of fortune John Hawkwood ('Giovanni Acuto'), a wise and courageous condottiere particularly well-versed in the arts of war - as the Latin inscription on the pedestal reads - who commanded the Florentine army from 1377 until his death in 1394. This is one of the most important examples of the painting of Paolo Uccello, the expression of a highly distinctive use of colour and the artist's personal study of perspective, which, quite removed from the scientific methods of Brunelleschi, aimed instead at an idealization of space and geometric forms.*

Interior - The austere Gothic interior of Santa Maria del Fiore is in the form of a Latin cross with nave and side aisles separated by massive clustered pilasters supporting imposing ogival vaults. Running along the nave is a gallery that continues in the transept and under the cupola. Many precious works were made in the course of the centuries to adorn the cathedral interior. Some of them, including the superb *Pietà* by Michelangelo and the *cantorie* (choir lofts) by Donatello and Luca Della Robbia, are at present housed in the Museo dell'Opera del Duomo. Others remain in their original position, including, in the left aisle, two interesting **frescoes** portraying equestrian monuments, one dedicated to John Hawkwood, the work of Paolo Uccello, the other to Niccolò da Tolentino, by Andrea del Castagno, as well as a painting representing *Dante explaining the Divine Comedy* by Domenico di Michelino. The polychrome *marble floor* was completed in various stages between 1526 and 1660 by numerous artists, but primarily by Baccio d'Agnolo.

Equestrian monument to Niccolò da Tolentino *by Andrea del Castagno.*

Dante and the Divine Comedy *by Domenico di Michelino; bottom, the interior of the cupola.*

Interior of the cupola - Brunelleschi's original project for the interior of the cupola of the Duomo provided for a mosaic decoration similar to that of the Baptistery, whose octagonal form had also been taken up in the construction of the dome. The mosaic decoration, however, was never made and for more than a century the cupola interior had nothing more than a simple whitewash finish. It was Cosimo I de' Medici who decided to have it frescoed and he entrusted the task of drawing up a detailed iconographical programme to Don Vincenzo Borghini, who according to the dictates of the Counter-Reformation elaborated the same subject that was represented in the Baptistery: the **Last Judgement.** For the execution of the cycle Cosimo summoned Vasari, who worked on the project from 1572 until his death in 1574. Francesco I de' Medici, who succeeded his father, commissioned Federico Zuccari to complete the frescoes left unfinished by his predecessor, which he did in 1579. The cycle unfolds in the eight segments of the cupola and on five levels one above the other. From the bottom upwards: *Hell* divided into seven areas corresponding to the seven *capital Sins;* the three *Theological Virtues* with *Gifts of the Spirit* and the *Beatitudes; Christ the Judge* with the *Hosts of Saints* and the *Elect* (including some members of the Medici family, such as Leo X): the *Angelic Orders* with instruments of the Passion; and finally *24 Elders of the Apocalypse.*

GIOTTO'S CAMPANILE

The campanile, or bell-tower, standing next to the Duomo was begun in 1334 on a design by Giotto, who supervised work on it until his death three years after the laying of the first stone. Giotto envisaged the campanile as an imposing but elegant square tower with corners reinforced with octagonal pilasters, but he succeeded in building only the **base section** where the entrance door is situated. Giotto's successor as city architect was Andrea Pisano, who worked on the project until 1348. In the band immediately above that built by Giotto, the artist continued the original structure, completing its decoration with two rows of **bas-relief panels** one above the other, the lower row being hexagonal in form, the upper row lozenge-shaped. The decorative panels constitute a complex iconographical cycle the subject of which is the life of Man, from the *Creation* to his *Civilization* through the practice of the *Arts* and *Sciences*, subject to the influence of the *Planets* and the exercise of the *Virtues*, by means of which the *Spirit*, sanctified by the *Sacraments*, bears fruit in the form of intellectual disciplines known as the *Liberal Arts*. The iconographical programme, founded on the process of human salvation according to Scholastic philosophy, is completed in the upper bands for the realization of which Andrea Pisano changed the original structure, dividing the four faces of the campanile with pairs of **pilaster strips** and decorating the spaces between them with Gothic niches, open in the lower band and blind in the one above. In the sixteen niches of the lower band statues of the *Prophets*, the *Sibyls* and *John the Baptist* were placed. Among those of the various Prophets, Donatello sculpted the statue of *Habakkuk*, the original of which is in the Museo dell'Opera del Duomo together with the original panels and other statues. Following the death of Andrea Pisano, Francesco Talenti continued work on the campanile which he finished in 1359. Talenti accentuated the vertical thrust of the building, inserting airy **arched windows** in pure Gothic style in the top three storeys. The soaring edifice, which was faced in polychrome marble and stands almost 85 metres high, was crowned by a cornice and **balustrade** resting on consoles and trefoil arches, similar to the one running along the outside of the adjoining cathedral.

BAPTISTERY

The Baptistery was constructed over the remains of an earlier Roman edifice, possibly the Praetorium or a temple dedicated to Mars, with building materials obtained from the abundant ruins that lay near the site. The Baptistery was originally built as a church dedicated to St John the Baptist between the 4th and the 5th century. The structure, with its octagonal plan, was faced externally with slabs of white and green marble arranged in a distinctive tripartite geometrical design. The height of the lower band was marked by a rectilinear trabeation, while the upper band was completed with round arches.

The Baptistry of San Giovanni.

The high attic, surmounted by a white pyramidal roof culminating in a **lantern**, and the rectangular **tribune** called the *scarsella* were added between the end of the 12th and the beginning of the 13th century. In 1059 the building was consecrated as a cathedral, and was used as such until 1128, when, with the enlargement of Santa Reparata, it went back to performing its earlier function as a baptistery. The octagonal form, which was taken up again in the cupola of the Duomo, has a specific religious significance associated with the ritual of baptism, by which the believer, having finished the "seven days" of his earthly life, can on the "eighth day" be reborn in Christ. This symbolism is echoed in the interior in the mosaics of the cupola. On the exterior are **three bronze doors**. The one on the *north side* was made by Lorenzo Ghiberti between 1403 and 1424 with *Stories of the New Testament*; the one on the *east side*, again by Ghiberti, is known as the *Gate of Paradise*; the one on the *south side*, the *South Door*, is the work of Andrea Pisano.

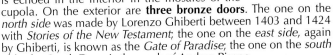

The **interior** of the Baptistery is an undivided octagonal space, richly adorned with polychrome marbles and mosaics with gold backgrounds, whose walls are divided into three superimposed orders. The first is divided by Corinthian columns and corner pilasters supporting a trabeation and **the women's gallery**, in its turn characterized by pairs of marble pilaster strips enclosing elegant double-arched bays and by a **parapet** with mosaics representing the *Prophets*. Above the women's gallery an attic with marble panels alternating with mosaics representing figures of *Saints* accentuates the insertion of the cupola. The original architectural arrangement of the interior, inspired both by Roman antiquity and by early medieval art, was subjected to substantial modifications in the course of time.

In 1202 a tribune known as the **'scarsella'** was added on the west side, the vault of which was decorated by the Franciscan monk Jacopo with mosaics representing a *wheel*, the symbol of Heavenly Jerusalem, with the *Agnus Dei* in the centre and all around *Prophets* and *Patriarchs* accompanied by the enthroned figures of the *Virgin and Child* and *St John the Baptist*. It was the same monk Jacopo who in the course of the 13th century began the mosaics of the cupola, which were executed by whole generations of artists. In 1577, for the baptism of Filippo, the son of Grand-duke Francesco I de' Medici, Buontalenti removed the choir in front of the scarsella and dismantled the **baptismal font** in the middle of the Baptistery. While modifications were being made to the original structure, the building was enriched inside with numerous works of art, some of which, like the *Mary Magdalen* by Donatello, are now in the Museo dell'Opera del Duomo. Donatello, together with Michelozzo, also executed the *tomb of the anti-Pope John XXIII*, which is still in its original position. The work was commissioned in 1421 by the heirs of the anti-Pope John XXIII, alias Cardinal Baldassarre Coscia, who died in Florence in 1419. The overall conception of the tomb is attributed to both artists, though they clearly worked on various parts of it individually. The effigy of the pope in gilded bronze is in fact the work of Donatello, while the relief under the sarcophagus representing the three *Theological Virtues* and the *Madonna and Child* in the shell niche under the marble baldachin seem to be by Michelozzo, although not all critics agree on this.

The **mosaics of the cupola** were begun towards the middle of the 13th century by the Franciscan monk Jacopo, who was also responsible for those of the scarsella. They were completed in the course of the following century by numerous artists belonging to Byzantine and Venetian artistic circles, who nonetheless elaborated designs by Tuscan artists like Coppo di Marcovaldo, who is attributed with the **Last Judgement**.

The iconographical cycle of the mosaics is developed, in a similar way to that of the frescoes in the cupola of the Duomo, in 5 bands one above the other, which are divided in turn into 8 segments. The highest band is made up of plant and animal symbolic motifs typical of the paleo-Christian tradition, while in the band below *Christ* and the *Angelic Orders* is represented. In the lower bands the cycle is divided into distinct parts: *Christ the Judge* and the *Last Judgement* in the three segments above the scarsella, while the remaining five segments, containing four bands, are occupied by the *Story of Genesis*, the *Story of Joseph*, the *Story of Christ* and the *Story of St John the Baptist*.

ANDREA PISANO
South Door
(1330-1336)

Commissioned by the Wool Merchants' Guild, which sponsored the building of the Baptistery, the door, modelled in bronze by Andrea Pisano in the first half of the 14th century, was originally placed on the east side of the building, from where it was subsequently removed to make way for Ghiberti's Gate of Paradise. The wings of the door are divided into 28 compartments containing as many quatrefoil panels representing the Stories of St John the Baptist, the person to whom the building was dedicated and the patron saint of Florence. The episode of the saint's decapitation is found repeated in the bronze sculpture above the architrave of the door, which portrays the Baptist kneeling between his executioner and Salome, all three made by Vincenzo Danti in 1571 to replace an earlier group representing the Baptism of Christ, now unfortunately lost.

Lorenzo GHIBERTI
Gate of Paradise
(1425-52)

The door on the east side of the Baptistery was described by Michelangelo as the Gate of Paradise, not only because of its beauty but also because of the symbolic importance of its position. Facing in the direction of the rising sun, the symbol of the birth of Christ, and also towards the entrance of the Duomo, it connects the two octagons (these too symbolic of the birth of Christ and human salvation) of the Baptistery and the cupola of the cathedral. The door was commissioned by the Merchants' Guild in 1425 to Ghiberti, who worked on it for almost thirty years with the assistance of talented artists like Michelozzo and Benozzo Gozzoli. Completed in 1452, the splendid door was positioned on the east side of the Baptistery, replacing the one made by Andrea Pisano which is now the South Door. The iconographical cycle represented in the decoration of the door wings is spread over 10 panels with bas-reliefs representing Stories from the Old Testament *enclosed within a frame of 24 niches made up of full-length statuettes reproducing* Biblical figures *alternating with 24 medallions containing small heads of* Artists, *including a self-portrait of Ghiberti himself. The original panels, made in embossed gilded bronze, are on display in the Museo dell'Opera del Duomo following a meticulous restoration.*

The Creation of Adam and Eve, Original Sin, The Fall from the Earthly Paradise.

The Sacrifice of Noah and his Family after Leaving the Ark, The Drunkenness of Noah.

The Birth of Esau and Jacob, Selling of the Birthright, Isaac and Esau Ordered to Go Hunting, Esau Hunting, Rebecca Advises Jacob, The Deceit of Isaac.

Moses Receives the Ten Commandments on Mount Sinai.

The Battle with the Philistines, The Slaying of Goliath.

The Work of the First Men, The Sacrifice of Cain and Abel, The Murder of Abel, The Lord Punishes Cain.

The Angels Appear to Abraham, The Sacrifice of Isaac.

Joseph Sold to the Merchants, The Discovery of the Golden Cup in Benjamin's Sack, Joseph Reveals Himself to his Brothers.

The People of Israel in Jordan, The Fall of Jericho.

Solomon and the Queen of Sheba

Gate of Paradise:

The Creation of Adam and Eve, Original Sin, The Fall from the Earthly Paradise.

The Battle with the Philistines, The Slaying of Goliath.

The interior of the Baptistry and the tomb of the anti-pope John XXIII.

The interior of the dome of the Baptistry and, bottom, the Loggia del Bigallo in Piazza San Giovanni.

LOGGIA DEL BIGALLO

The loggia, built on a design by Alberto Arnoldi, was commissioned in the middle of the 14th century by the Compagnia della Misericordia, a charitable institution dedicated to helping orphans and abandoned children. In 1425 the Compagnia della Misericordia was replaced by the Compagnia del Bigallo, founded in the middle of the 13th century by St Peter Martyr and administering various hospitals and a famous orphanage, to which the loggia still belongs. Its exterior, built in marble richly decorated with reliefs representing biblical figures, appears as the right-angled union of two elegant round arches closed by railings and small gates. On the upper floor, whose exterior is characterized by refined Gothic two-arched bays, are various rooms, including a large room once used for the meetings of members of the Compagnia del Bigallo. Today it contains works of art of considerable value linked to the history of this charitable institution.

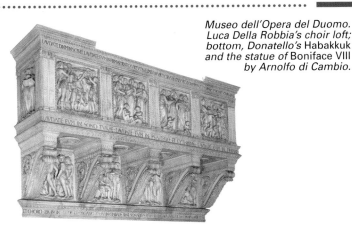

*Museo dell'Opera del Duomo.
Luca Della Robbia's choir loft;
bottom, Donatello's* Habakkuk
and the statue of Boniface VIII
by Arnolfo di Cambio.

MUSEO DELL'OPERA DEL DUOMO

The museum, housed in a building behind the cathedral, contains numerous works, particularly sculptures, belonging to the various decorative phases of the monumental complex formed by the Duomo, the Baptistery and the Campanile. On the ground floor, in the **Room of the old facade of the Duomo**, are the sculptures removed after the 1587 demolition of the original facade designed by Arnolfo di Cambio. Particularly striking are the *Madonna and Child* and the *statue of Boniface VIII*, both works by Arnolfo. On the floor above in the **Room of the Cantorie** are the two *Cantorie* by Luca Della Robbia and Donatello, as well as the *16 original statues* once occupying the niches of the Campanile, now replaced by copies. Especially noteworthy is Donatello's statue of the prophet *Habakkuk*, popularly known as 'Lo Zuccone' (the great bald-headed one'). The museum also houses works removed from their original positions many centuries ago and recovered later from Florentine palaces and gardens, but also works which until a few decades ago decorated the Duomo, like the *Pietà* by Michelangelo, or the Baptistery, like the *Mary Magdalen* by Donatello.

DONATELLO
Mary Magdalen
(1453-55)

The emaciated figure of Mary Magdalen, which Donatello modelled with extreme realism, expresses the abandonment of the material world and the attainment of spiritual ecstasy through penance and contrition. The beauty of the body, now cancelled by privation, has been sublimated in the beauty of a soul which through pain is redeemed and reconciled with God. After a careful restoration the wooden statue, which once stood in the Baptistery, is now on display in the Museo dell'Opera del Duomo.

The choir loft by Donatello.

MICHELANGELO
Pietà
(1550-53)

This marble sculpture, which Michelangelo never completed, was, in the artist's intentions, supposed to have adorned his own funerary chapel in Santa Maria Maggiore in Rome. In actual fact it never left Florence, and only in the 18th century was it set up in one of the chapels of the left tribune of the cathedral, from where it was removed in more recent times to its present position in the Museo dell'Opera del Duomo. In the centre of the group is the figure of the dead Christ supported by Nicodemus, in whom it is traditionally believed the sculptor portrayed his own likeness, by the Madonna and by Mary Magdalen, finished by one of Michelangelo's pupils. The figure of Christ, whose arm (later restored) and left leg were destroyed by the artist in a fit of rage, is, with its modelling, the fulcrum of the composition. The unfinshed state of the sculpture confers to the whole a heightened sense of dramatic force.

BASILICA OF SAN LORENZO

This, the oldest church in Florence, was originally built outside the first ring of city walls and consecrated by Ambrose in 393. Around the year 1000, with the expansion of medieval Florence, the early construction was enlarged and renewed in typically Romanesque style. The present building is the result of a much later intervention, financed largely by the Medici family, who in 1419 commissioned Filippo Brunelleschi to supervise the work of building a basilica that would be completely original from an architectural point of view. Brunelleschi worked on it in several stages over a period of more than twenty years up to his death in 1446. One of his pupils, Antonio Manetti, completed the work of building San Lorenzo, which went on until 1460. The **facade** remained to be done, and for its execution Michelangelo was summoned. In 1518 the artist drew up an ambitious design that found partial expression inside the building with the construction of the inner facade balcony for the exposition of relics; on the outside the church remained, as it remains today, totally without a facade.

At the side of the basilica, and confirming the conventual origin of the complex, is an elegant **cloister** with a double row of arches leading to the **Biblioteca Laurenziana.**

The **interior** of the basilica is one of the most harmonious creations of Florentine Renaissance architecture. The building, a Latin cross, consists of a nave and side aisles separated by Corinthian columns in pietra serena (used for all the architectural mouldings) supporting round arches. Above the nave is a coffered ceiling, while the side aisles, with pilaster strips framing the chapel entrances, are covered by cloister vaults. In the nave are *two bronze pulpits* by Donatello, who also worked on the decoration of the **Old Sacristy**, entered from the left side of the transept. Opposite, on the opposite side of the transept, is the entrance to the **New Sacristy**, where the Medici tombs are.

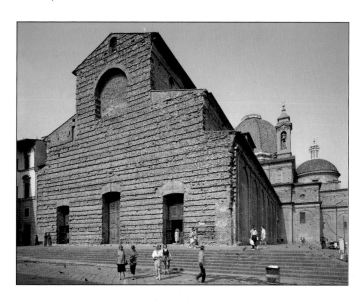

The interior of the church of San Lorenzo.

These *two bronze pulpits* were the last works of Donatello. They were in fact only partly executed by the artist, being almost entirely finished by some of his pupils who faithfully followed their master's original designs. Conceived in the form of classical arches supported by marble columns, they were mounted on the occasion of the visit to Florence of Pope Leo X. Almost all the bronze bas-reliefs reproduce scenes of Christ's Passion.

One of the two bronze pulpits by Donatello.

MEDICI CHAPELS

The complex known as the Medici Chapels is the mausoleum of the Medici family and at the same time one of the most important monuments to the glory of the powerful Florentine dynasty to whose fortunes the history of the city remained inseparably linked for centuries. It consists of two main parts: one, the **Chapel of the Princes,** architecturally independent of the adjoining Basilica of San Lorenzo, and the other, the **New Sacristy**, more closely connected to the structure of the church, which is reached both from the interior of the basilica and from the Chapel of the Princes. There is also a third area, a vast *crypt*, in the pavement of which are the tombstones of various Medici princes. The crypt continues under the basilica and houses the tombs of Cosimo il Vecchio and Donatello, as well as those of various members of the Lorraine family.

The statue of Giuliano de' Medici, Duke of Nemours, and the dome of the Cappella dei Principi.

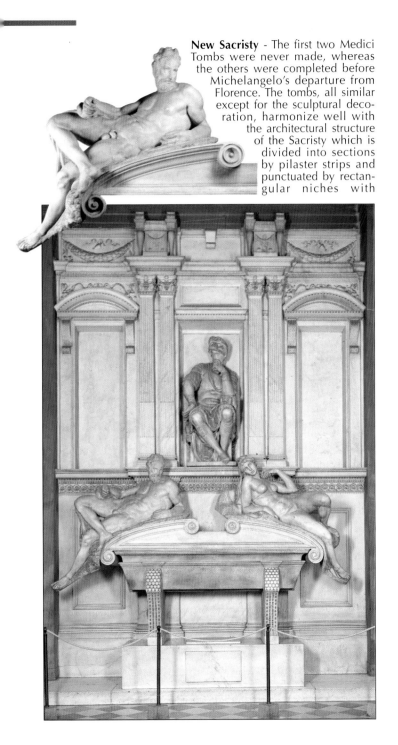

New Sacristy - The first two Medici Tombs were never made, whereas the others were completed before Michelangelo's departure from Florence. The tombs, all similar except for the sculptural decoration, harmonize well with the architectural structure of the Sacristy which is divided into sections by pilaster strips and punctuated by rectangular niches with curved pediments.

The **Tomb of Lorenzo**, Duke of Urbino, grandson of Lorenzo il Magnifico and nephew of Leo X, houses in the central niche, above the sarcophagus, the *Statue of the Duke*, who is portrayed ideally in a contemplative pose. On the volutes of the funerary urn below are two other symmetrically arranged statues with a purely allegorical significance: *Dawn*, who reluctantly rouses from nocturnal slumber, and *Twilight*, who falls asleep pervaded by melancholy.

The **Tomb of Giuliano**, Duke of Nemours, the third-born son of Lorenzo il Magnifico, has on the urn the powerful and dramatic statues of *Day* and *Night*, which together with the previous parts of the day lend meaning to the complex allegory of the transience and insubstantiality of human life. The *Statue of Duke Giuliano* has the idealized features of a bold young warrior. The remains of Lorenzo il Magnifico and his brother Giuliano were arranged by Vasari in a simple tomb, on which the architect placed Michelangelo's solemn but vigorous statue representing the **Madonna and Child**, surrounded by the portraits of *Saints Cosmas and Damian*, executed by two pupils of Michelangelo on a design by the master

Facing page:
Michelangelo's tomb of Lorenzo, Duke of Urbino and, top, Dusk.

On this page: Dawn, Night, *and* Day *by Michelangelo.*

The Chapel of the Princes and, left, the tomb of Giuliano, Duke of Nemours.

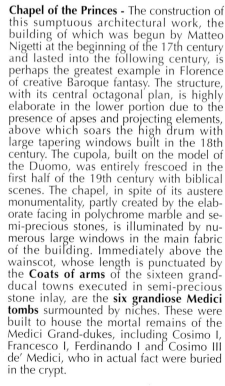

Chapel of the Princes - The construction of this sumptuous architectural work, the building of which was begun by Matteo Nigetti at the beginning of the 17th century and lasted into the following century, is perhaps the greatest example in Florence of creative Baroque fantasy. The structure, with its central octagonal plan, is highly elaborate in the lower portion due to the presence of apses and projecting elements, above which soars the high drum with large tapering windows built in the 18th century. The cupola, built on the model of the Duomo, was entirely frescoed in the first half of the 19th century with biblical scenes. The chapel, in spite of its austere monumentality, partly created by the elaborate facing in polychrome marble and semi-precious stones, is illuminated by numerous large windows in the main fabric of the building. Immediately above the wainscot, whose length is punctuated by the **Coats of arms** of the sixteen grand-ducal towns executed in semi-precious stone inlay, are the **six grandiose Medici tombs** surmounted by niches. These were built to house the mortal remains of the Medici Grand-dukes, including Cosimo I, Francesco I, Ferdinando I and Cosimo III de' Medici, who in actual fact were buried in the crypt.

PALAZZO MEDICI RICCARDI

The palace was built to be the residence of the Medici family in accordance with the wishes of Cosimo il Vecchio. He initially commissioned the project to Brunelleschi, who planned the construction of an imposing edifice in Piazza San Lorenzo. But Cosimo, who preferred the residence to be of a more modest size and situated in a less prominent position, chose what was then called Via Larga as the site on which to build the palace, and

entrusted the project to Michelozzo, who had faithfully followed him in exile to Venice in 1433.

Michelozzo, undoubtedly keeping Brunelleschi's original design in mind, built the palace between 1444 and 1464. It was of equal height and width, and arranged on three storeys around a **central courtyard** with classical columns, a courtyard subsequently adorned with bas-reliefs and statues, including the *Orpheus* by Baccio Bandinelli which was moved here from the stairway of Palazzo Vecchio.

On the ground floor Michelozzo lightened the powerful external walls in rusticated pietra forte by building a loggia on the corner, next to the imposing entrance door. In 1517 the loggia was walled up and embellished with large pedimented windows which are attributed to Michelangelo. The first floor has a smoother rusticated surface than the ground floor and a row of elegant round-arched mullioned windows, which are repeated on the top floor whose wall surface is completely smooth. The Medici **coat of arms** was mounted on the corner of the building at the first floor level. Crowning the facade the traditional battlement was replaced by a classical cornice with sculpted consoles. The palace was inhabited by the main branch of the family until the time of Cosimo I de' Medici, who in 1540 transferred the family residence to Palazzo Vecchio. The palace in Via Larga continued to be used by members of the minor branches of the family, widows and unmarried women. In 1655 the palace passed to the marquises of the Riccardi family who between 1670 and 1720 extended the building both at the back and along the main

Left and on this page, details of the frescoes by Benozzo Gozzoli, in the chapel of Palazzo Medici Riccardi, of the Procession of the Magi.

39

Benozzo Gozzoli's frescoes in the chapel
of Palazzo Medici Riccardi.

facade, where 7 bays on each floor and the entrance to the stables were added, thus altering significantly Michelozzo's original building. The interior, which had already been modified in the 16th century, was also extensively rebuilt, with the exception of the lovely chapel. Like Palazzo Medici, the **chapel** too was built in the 15th century by Michelozzo, who was also responsible for the splendid coffered ceiling and precious floor inlaid with precious polychrome marbles. The room is rectangular and has a square apse framed by voluted pilasters with Corinthian capitals. It was frescoed between 1459 and 1460 by Benozzo Gozzoli, who painted the *Procession of the Magi to Bethlehem*.
In the 19th century the palace came into the possession of the Lorraine family, after which it was taken over by the municipal authorities to house the offices of the Prefecture.

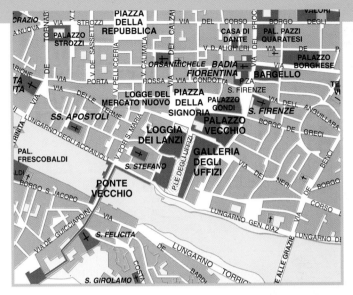

Piazza della Signoria, the Uffizi, and Ponte Vecchio

Just a short way from the Duomo is the political center of the city: Piazza della Signoria. Packed with people at all hours of the day, it unfolds like a broad open-air gallery in which even the statues symbolically allude to episodes of the city's civil history. Facing directly on the square are the three elegant arches of the Loggia dei Lanzi and Palazzo Vecchio, the seat of city government since 1878 and dubbed "Vecchio" when the Medici family abandoned it to move

to their new home, Palazzo Pitti. We owe the layout of its monumental interior (where, of the twenty rooms open to the public, we recommend visiting at least the precious Sala dei Gigli) to the genius of Giorgio Vasari, the multifaceted artist who left his mark on the Cinquecento as architect, painter, and writer. His masterpiece: the complex of the Uffizi, with the Vasari Corridor. Today, the light-filled rooms of the former "Offices" are host to the world's oldest art gallery. The "secret" Corridor starts at the Uffizi, runs over Ponte Vecchio, and ends at Palazzo Pitti. Reservations are required to view the works on exhibit in the Corridor and the unusual view of the Arno from above Ponte Vecchio. A word to the wise: unless you make reservations in advance, a visit to the Galleria degli Uffizi can mean long waiting lines!

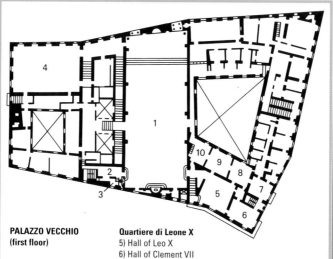

PALAZZO VECCHIO
(first floor)

1) Salone dei Cinquecento
2) Studiolo di Francesco I
3) Tesoretto di Cosimo I
4) Salone dei Duecento

Quartiere di Leone X
5) Hall of Leo X
6) Hall of Clement VII
7) Hall of Giovanni dalle Bande Nere
8) Hall of Cosimo the Elder
9) Hall of Lorenzo the Magnificent
10) Hall of Cosimo I

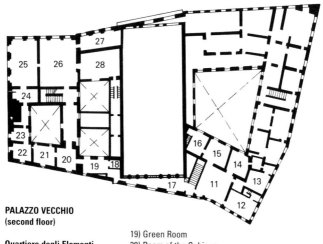

PALAZZO VECCHIO
(second floor)

Quartiere degli Elementi
11) Hall of the Elements
12) Terrace of Saturn
13) Room of Hercules
14) Room of Jupiter
15) Room of Cybele or Opis
16) Room of Ceres
17) "Ballatoio"
Quartiere di Eleonora di Toledo
18) Eleonora's Chapel

19) Green Room
20) Room of the Sabines
21) Room of Esther
22) Room of Penelope
23) Room of Gualdrada
Quartiere dei Priori
24) Cappella della Signoria
25) Audience Hall
26) Sala dei Gigli
27) Chancellery
28) Wardrobe

PIAZZA DELLA SIGNORIA

Piazza della Signoria is the centre of Florentine civic life. It was created in the area occupied in the 13th century by the houses of some powerful Ghibelline families, including the Uberti and the Foraboschi, which were razed to the ground by the Guelf faction after the battle of Benevento. Part of the area around a surviving tower belonging to the Foraboschi family was occupied by **Palazzo Vecchio**, which was built with an asymmetrical ground-plan due to the nearby presence of the old church of San Piero Scheraggio. The church was later demolished to make space for the Uffizi. The appearance of the square, which was originally called the Piazza dei Priori, changed various times during the course of the centuries. In the middle of the 14th century the Tettoia dei Pisani was built along the west side, only to be demolished in 1870. At the end of the 15th century the **Loggia dei Lanzi** was built on the south side, and was enriched with precious sculptures during the 16th century. Other sculptures decorated the square in the same years. The steps in front of Palazzo Vecchio were used to accommodate *Hercules and Cacus* by Baccio Bandinelli and the *David* by Michelangelo, the latter being replaced by a copy in 1873 when the original was taken to the Accademia. On the far left of the steps Ammannati erected the **Fountain of Neptune**, and the part of the square nearest the Tribunale della Mercatanzia became the site for the *Equestrian Monument to Cosimo I* by Giambologna.

A view of Piazza della Signoria.

ARNOLFO'S TOWER

Arnolfo di Cambio built the tower of Palazzo Vecchio on top of the old *Torre della Vacca* of the Foraboschi family, the only surviving tower of those houses which in the 13th century occupied the area and were demolished during feuds between Guelfs and Ghibellines. The tower is 94 metres high. At the front it rests on the gallery, whose characteristic decoration is repeated higher up, though with variations like the swallow-tail crenellation, typical of the Ghibelline faction, and the supporting pointed arches. The belfry above is crowned by yet another crenellation and surmounted by a bronze pinnacle of the mid-15th century ending in a pole with a lily and lion rampant, emblems of the city of Florence.

Fountain of Neptune - The fountain (1563-75) by Bartolomeo Ammannati, is dedicated to the sea-god Neptune, who stands with three tritons on a light chariot drawn by four horses in the middle of a basin. The enormous marble statue of the god, which Ammannati sculpted with a certain carelessness for the proportions, came in for a fair amount of criticism by the people of Florence who jokingly nicknamed it "Il Biancone" (the big white one). The bronze statues along the edge of the basin representing nymphs and other mythological creatures in Neptune's cortège, on which Giambologna probably worked, are rather more accomplished.

The Fountain of Neptune by Ammannati.

Equestrian Monument to Cosimo I - This bronze monument by Giambologna (1594) portrays the stately figure of Grand-duke Cosimo I de' Medici - the great patron of the arts who was responsible for glorifying both the square and Palazzo Vecchio looking onto it - sitting solemnly on horse-

back as if to observe the various masterpieces commissioned by him. On the base of the monument are three bronze bas-reliefs portraying *Cosimo's entrance into Siena, The conferment of the grand-ducal title on Cosimo by the Tuscan Senate* and *The conferment of the grand-ducal insignia by Pius V*, the salient episodes of a triumphant rise that led Cosimo to attain the highest office of the Florentine state, of which he is quite rightly considered to be the founding father.

LOGGIA DEI LANZI

The loggia was built on a design by Orcagna between 1376 and 1382 by the architects Benci di Cione and Simone Talenti to house the most eminent Florentine government officials, including the Priors, and for receiving important visitors to the city. It was called the loggia 'dei Lanzi' because in the 16th century Grand-duke Cosimo I de' Medici stationed a band of German mercenary soldiers called lansquenets here as his bodyguard.

The elegant airy construction is a splendid example of Florentine Gothic, combining Romanesque round arches with soaring clustered columns and a refined crowning decoration of trefoil arches typical of the international Gothic style.

Initially the only decoration in the Loggia consisted of various lobed spandrels portraying the *Virtues*, works executed by Agnolo Gaddi at the end of the 14th century.

When there was no longer any need for the building to be used for military purposes, Cosimo I had it fitted with partitions and transformed the spaces thus created into workshops for artists, who

Benvenuto CELLINI
Perseus
(1545-54)

The Greek hero Perseus, son of Danae and Zeus, was challenged by the tyrant of the island of Seriphos, Polydectes, to slay the Medusa, a terrible serpent-headed female creature who had the power to turn anyone who looked at her into stone. Assisted by Hermes and Athena, Perseus succeeded in the undertaking and with his dreadful trophy proceeded to free Andromeda, whom he later married, from a horrifying sea monster. In this bronze statue, Cellini's undisputed masterpiece, the hero is represented standing triumphantly over the vanquished and headless Medusa. In the statuettes of the elaborate pedestal the artist then portrayed the other characters in the legend of Perseus: Danae, holding her baby boy, Zeus, Athena and Hermes, and in the bas-relief on the base, Perseus freeing Andromeda. The work was commissioned by Grand-duke Cosimo I de' Medici and symbolizes the triumph and glory of Florence and the Medici dynasty.

The Loggia dei Lanzi.

were then commissioned to execute colossal works glorifying the Medici dynasty. Only subsequently were various classical and modern statues set up here, like the *Perseus* by Benvenuto Cellini and the *Rape of the Sabines* by Giambologna, which gave the loggia its present appearance as an open-air art gallery.

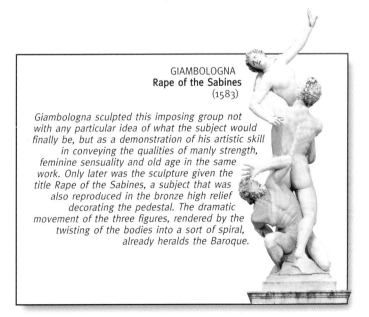

GIAMBOLOGNA
Rape of the Sabines
(1583)

Giambologna sculpted this imposing group not with any particular idea of what the subject would finally be, but as a demonstration of his artistic skill in conveying the qualities of manly strength, feminine sensuality and old age in the same work. Only later was the sculpture given the title Rape of the Sabines, a subject that was also reproduced in the bronze high relief decorating the pedestal. The dramatic movement of the three figures, rendered by the twisting of the bodies into a sort of spiral, already heralds the Baroque.

PALAZZO VECCHIO

Palazzo Vecchio was the most important public building of medieval Florence. Its original nucleus was built between 1299 and 1314 to house the offices of the Priors, the highest-ranking officials of the Florentine city government. Arnolfo di Cambio was commissioned to supervise the building and he chose as the site the area where the houses of the Ghibelline family of the Uberti had once stood, houses that had been demolished by the opposing Guelf faction. Arnolfo built Palazzo Vecchio on an assymetrical ground-plan around the surviving Torre della Vacca belonging to the Foraboschi family, onto which in 1310 he built the tower we see today. Originally the palace was built around a central courtyard with the rooms arranged on three floors. When the Duke of Athens came to power in Florence the original structure was subjected to various modifications, which were followed a century and a half later by further alterations suggested by Savonarola and carried out by Cronaca. Cronaca extended the palace by adding another courtyard, later called the **Cortile della Dogana**, with the Sala del Consiglio Generale del Popolo, the present Salone dei Cinquecento, above it. After the fall of the Florentine republic and the Medici family's rise to power in the city, the glorious building became the residence of Grand-duke Cosimo I de' Medici, who having left the ancestral home of Palazzo Medici commissioned Vasari to enlarge and embellish the new residence. Between 1540 and 1543 Vasari incorporated various buildings adjacent to the Arnolfian construction, thereby creating a majestic complex with monumental quarters. The first floor of Vasari's building housed Cosimo's apartment, whose rooms were each dedicated to a member of the Medici family. The second floor housed the Quartiere degli Elementi, whose rooms each centered around a different god of classical mythology, as did those of the adjoining Loggiati. Lastly, the old Quartiere dei Priori was converted into the Quartiere di Eleonora, the apartments of Cosimo's wife. The only other Grand-duke besides Cosimo who inhabited this princely residence was Francesco I de' Medici, for whom Vasari constructed the celebrated Studiolo. Palazzo Vecchio was in fact less popular than Palazzo Pitti, which, following the construction of the Uffizi, Cosimo had connected to the residence of Piazza Signoria by means of the **Vasari Corridor**. Although they chose to live in the new residence on the other side of the Arno, the Medici did not stop making improvements to Palazzo Vecchio, whose rear

section was modified by Buontalenti at the end of the 16th century. When the rule of the Lorraine, who succeeded the Medici, came to an end, and Florence became the capital of the Italian kingdom, Palazzo Vecchio housed the Chamber of Deputies. Today it is the seat of the municipal government.

Facade - The austere Arnolfian facade is built in rusticated pietra forte. It is divided into three horizontal storeys by two narrow string-courses and there are two rows of graceful two-arched bays with marble decoration on which the symbols of the Cross and the Lily are represented. Crowning the upper storey is a battlemented gallery supported by brackets and round arches, within which the **nine emblems** of the Florentine republic were frescoed in the 15th century. At the beginning of the 16th century the entrance portal was decorated with an emblem bearing **Christ's initials between two gold lions** and an inscription inspired by Savonarola which Cosimo I changed into the present one praising Christ - "King of kings and Lord of the mighty".

Interior - The first impression of the interior of Palazzo Vecchio we get from the old **Arnolfian courtyard,** which in 1470 Michelozzo modified by adding a portico. The austere Renaissance courtyard was instead embellished by Cosimo I de' Medici, who in 1565, on the occasion of his son's marriage to Joan of Austria, had the columns and pillars decorated with stuccoes on a gold background and the walls frescoed with views of the Habsburg dominions. In the middle of the courtyard, in place of the old well, the Grand-duke placed an elegant **fountain** decorated with a *Putto with a dolphin* by Verrocchio, the original of which is in a room of the palace. On the first floor is the **Salone dei Cinquecento** (Hall of the Five Hundred), originally built by Cronaca to house the Consiglio Generale del Popolo - the governing body of the Floren-

Top, Verrocchio's Putto with a Dolphin, *a copy of which decorates the fountain in the courtyard designed by Michelozzo; bottom, the Salone dei Cinquecento.*

On the facing page, the Studiolo of Francesco I.

tine republic created by Savonarola in 1494 - and raised in 1563 by Vasari, who built a new coffered ceiling richly decorated and painted with *Allegories and Stories of Florence and the Medici Family*. The walls of the hall, which were supposed to have been frescoed by Leonardo and Michelangelo, were instead painted by Vasari with *Battle Scenes*. The hall, which in the Medici period was used for receptions and public celebrations, houses numerous sculptural works including Michelangelo's *Genius of Victory* and various statues representing the *Labours of Hercules* by Vincenzo de' Rossi. The Salone dei Cinquecento leads into the **Studiolo di Francesco I**, an elegant room created by Vasari and richly decorated by some of the greatest Florentine artists of the 16th century, who produced a complex iconographical programme combining mythological and alchemical elements in a sort of intricate allegory of human knowledge and progress. The adjoining **Quartiere di Leone X**, today occupied by the mayor's offices, has superb decorations by Vasari, including a fresco depicting the *Siege of Florence*, which adorns one of the walls in the Sala di Clemente VII. The second floor of the palace, occupied at the front by the old

Hercules and Diomedes *by Vincenzo de' Rossi.*

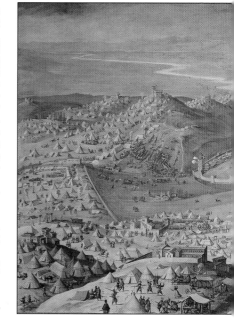

DONATELLO
Judith and Holofernes
(1455-60)
Sala dei Gigli

This dramatic bronze statue, thought to be one of the artist's last works, shows the biblical heroine in the act of severing the head from the body of Holofernes, the general in the army of the Assyrian king Nebuchadnezzar who had laid siege to Judith's native town of Bethulia. The statue has had a somewhat unsettled life. It was initially placed on a fountain in Palazzo Medici, but was removed and set up in public after the first expulsion of the Medici family from Florence. It was moved again several times and finally ended up first under the Loggia dei Lanzi, then on the steps in front of Palazzo Vecchio, and lastly inside the palace where it now is following the splendid restoration carried out between 1980 and 1986. The three reliefs with Bacchic scenes on the triangular base allude to the drunkenness of Holofernes. In order to kill the enemy leader, Judith had in fact offered herself up as a prisoner; after being led to the general's tent she offered him wine and then heroically decapitated her drunken victim.

Quartiere dei Priori, starts with the **Sala dei Gigli**, built by Benedetto da Maiano. The magnificent coffered ceiling in this room, which rests on a fascia with paired lions holding the nine emblems of the Florentine republic, was built by Benedetto's brother Giuliano da Maiano. The room gets its name from the French lilies adorning the walls, one of which is further embellished with *frescoes* by Ghirlandaio portraying figures from Roman history with St Zenobius in the centre, enthroned between St Lawrence and St Stephen. The splendid decorations act as a frame for the original bronze statue of *Judith and Holofernes,* a masterpiece by Donatello. From here a door leads into the **Cancelleria**, where Niccolò Machiavelli worked as a secretary. The **Sala dell'Udienza** is connected to the Sala dei Gigli by means of a white marble doorway whose lunette contains the 15th-century statue of *Justice* by Giuliano and Benedetto da Maiano. From this room we enter the **Cappella della Signoria**, built in 1511, where the Priors gathered in the morning to attend Mass and read pages from the Gospel and Justinian's Digests, these symbolizing respectively divine and human law. The chapel was dedicated to St Anne and the Virgin, who are represented in the *Sacra Conversazione* by Mariano da Pescia above the altar. The rooms adjoining the chapel, once occupied by the Priors, were converted by Vasari into the **Quartiere di Eleonora di Toledo**. Eleonora slept in the *Camera Verde* whose vault is decorated with elegant grotesques. A small passage leads to the **Quartiere degli Elementi,** built by Giovan Battista del Tasso in the middle of the 16th century. The apartment gets its name from the *Sala degli Elementi*, whose walls Vasari frescoed with allegories of the four natural elements: *Air, Water, Earth* and *Fire*. The other rooms are dedicated to the Olympian gods: the **Camera di Ercole** which contains a particularly interesting ebony cabinet decorated with semi-precious stone intarsia, a German work of the 17th century donated to Grand-duke Ferdinando II de' Medici, and the **Loggia di Giunone** which houses Verrocchio's original *Putto with a Dolphin*.

Sala di Clemente VII. Vasari's reconstruction of the Siege of Florence *by the Imperial troops of Charles V in 1529-30 offers a minutely detailed record of 16th-century Florence.*

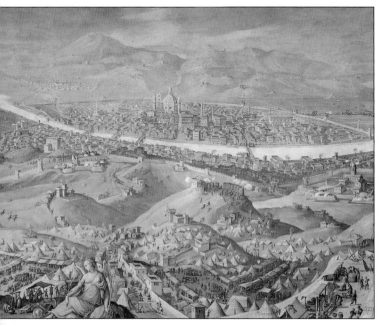

VASARI CORRIDOR

This raised passageway, commissioned by Cosimo de' Medici, was built by Vasari in only five months in 1565. Its purpose was to connect the Uffizi with Palazzo Pitti on the south side of the river, the residence Cosimo had chosen to live in during the final years of his grand-ducal reign. Resting on a series of arches the corridor crosses the river Arno above Ponte Vecchio, and after going round the Torre dei Mannelli and past the church of Santa Felicita, finally reaches Palazzo Pitti. On display in it are many works of the 17th and 18th century and a large collection of self-portraits by artists who lived between the 16th and 19th centuries.

Top, a view of the Vasari Corridor where it joins Ponte Vecchio; bottom, a portion of the Uffizi overlooking the Arno.

UFFIZI

The Palazzo degli Uffizi was commissioned to Giorgio Vasari by Cosimo I de' Medici in 1560, and completed, according to the original project, by Alfonso Parigi and Bernardo Buontalenti in 1580. It was built next to Palazzo Vecchio, following the latter's enlargement, to house the offices of the city magistracies. The palace of the Uffizi is a long, U-shaped structure, almost a theatrical enclosure, which extends as far as the north bank of the Arno. Building it involved sacrificing the glorious old church of **San Piero Scheraggio**, which was partly demolished and partly incorporated into the new edifice. On the ground floor Vasari built lofty arcades supported by alternating Doric columns and pilasters and above them a loggia, which initially had no specific use. It was Cosimo's successor, Francesco I de' Medici, who decided that the loggia should have the present-day function of a Gallery, and he commissioned Buontalenti to build the **Tribune**, where the Grandduke ammassed numerous precious objects and ancient medals. Francesco also set out the first corridor of the gallery, placing in it the Medici family's collection of Greek and Roman statues, from which the *Galleria delle Statue* gets its name.

After Francesco's death, Ferdinando I de' Medici had the classical statues of Villa Medici transferred from Rome to Florence, thus further enriching the collection, to which were soon added also the finest pieces from the Medici Armoury and a collection of Mathematical Instruments. The Gallery benefited from other substantial acquisitions in the 17th century, notably that of the wife of Ferdinando II de' Medici, Vittoria della Rovere, whose dowry contained the immense patrimony of her grandfather Federico, Duke of Urbino, including precious works by Raphael and Titian. The other important acquisition enriching the Medici collections was Cardinal Leopold's bequest to his nephew Cosimo III de' Medici, who built new rooms in order to accommodate it, and constructed a new and more monumental entrance to the Uffizi. Cosimo's daughter Anna Maria Ludovica, last of the Medici and widow of the Elector Palatine, added works by German and Flemish masters, and through a family Pact of 1737 settled that the art collections belonging to her family be left to the city of Florence. The **Galleria degli Uffizi** thus became the city's first art museum, a museum that in the following decades continued to grow and inspired the creation of other prestigious Florentine museums.

The loggia of the Uffizi in a detail of The Goldsmith's Workshop *by Alessandro Fei (ca. 1570).*

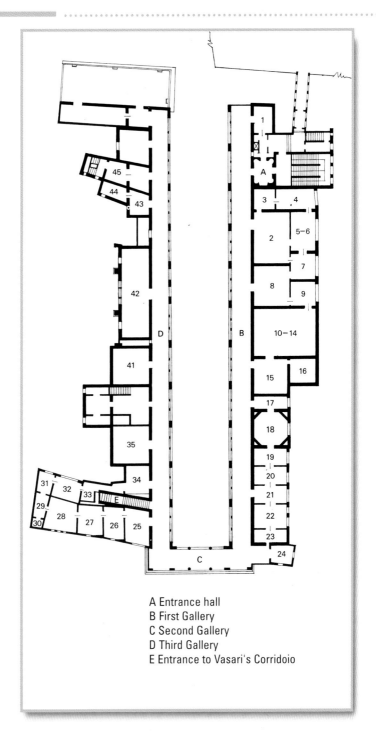

A Entrance hall
B First Gallery
C Second Gallery
D Third Gallery
E Entrance to Vasari's Corridoio

GALLERIA DEGLI UFFIZI

The Museum of the Uffizi Gallery has known a period of unbroken development since the 16th century, one marked by successive acquisitions of works and collections. This has involved the progressive enlargement of the space required to house them. Thus, the area of the museum, which in the past occupied only that part named 'The Gallery', was extended to incorporate also part of the Vasari Corridor and the Tribune. In 1988 the rooms of the ground floor and the first floor (originally used as offices of the Signoria) became available following the transferral of the State Archives, at the Uffizi since 1852, to a new site. As part of the **"Nuovi Uffizi"** project, the subsequent triplication of space enables the numerous works kept in the storerooms of the museum to be displayed.

In the rooms the paintings and sculptures are arranged chronologically and are displayed in clearly defined sections which correspond to the centuries of their respective production. Thus it is possible to admire, in succession, the sections dedicated to the **Painting of the 13th and 14th century**, the **Painting of the 15th century**, **North European Painting**, the **Tribune**, **Painting of the 16th century** and **Painting of the 17th and 18th century**.

Painting of the 13th and 14th century, p. 56

Painting of the 15th century, p. 59

North European Painting, p. 70

The Tribune, p. 71

Painting of the 16th century, p. 73

Painting of the 17th and 18th century, p. 76

Painting of the 13th and 14th century

The history of Italian and particularly Tuscan art in the 13th and 14th centuries is the history of an evolution from forms ideologically and technically independent of the Byzantine tradition to the more humanly concrete and spatially defined forms of Western art. Mosaic and fresco painting were still the most commonly used techniques during this period, although painting on wood, in which colours were applied in tempera, was more and more widely adopted. Generally speaking, however, modes of pictorial expression evolved imperceptibly and even within mosaic and fresco cycles dramatic and popularesque elements introducing a more concrete sense of reality became increasingly common. In the same way painting on wood continued in its conquest of human values, portraying actions and sentiments that could be fully understood, particularly with the help of a progressively defined sense of space. The same subjects, given their almost exclusively ecclesiastical destination, appeared again and again: Crucifixes in which Christ was presented as *triumphans*, but also and increasingly often as *patiens*, Enthroned Madonnas, and large figures of Saints surrounded by small scenes depicting episodes from their lives. Among the most important artists who distinguished themselves in the field of the arts during these two centuries were Cimabue, Giotto and his followers.

GIOTTO
Ognissanti Madonna
(ca. 1303)

This work was executed for the high altar of the church of Ognissanti.
In this painting, which for reasons of style can be placed between the frescoes of Assisi and those of the Scrovegni Chapel in Padua, Giotto broke with the Byzantine tradition and drew instead on classical art and culture. The ample spatial structure is now confidently three-dimensional, as we can see from the perspective of the throne and the staggered positions of the angels.
(Room 2)

DUCCIO DI BUONINSEGNA
Rucellai Madonna
(1285)

The Rucellai Madonna is an extremely important work belonging to Duccio's early period. This painting, which was for a long time attributed to Cimabue, recalls in the faces of the angels and the Child the Santa Trinita Maestà, but the delicate spirituality, the lightness of the bodies and the lively decoration, create a pensive Madonna, a fragile Child, and angels absorbed in aristocratic contemplation. It is less dramatic than Cimabue's Madonna, but no less moving or emotionally charged.
(Room 2)

Ambrogio LORENZETTI
Presentation in the Temple
(1342)

Attributable to Lorenzetti on the basis of documented payments dating from 1339 and 1340, this work is also signed and dated. It is the central part of a triptych, whose side panels with Saints Crescentius and Michael Archangel are now lost. Ambrogio Lorenzetti's poetic imagination is very apparent in this work, in which the figures, painted with a meticulous, analytical care, stand out against an elegant, finely decorated architectural structure.
(Room 3)

Pietro LORENZETTI
Madonna and Child Enthroned with Angels
(14th C.)

In this work, as in all his Madonnas, Pietro Lorenzetti emphasizes the human dimension of the relationship between Mother and Child, a rapport which the other figures portrayed are drawn to share in.
(Room 3)

Taddeo GADDI
Madonna and Child Enthroned with Angels and Saints
(1355)

This painting and the small Berlin triptych of 1353 are the only surviving signed and dated works by Taddeo Gaddi, works that are therefore highly important in establishing a point of reference for this master's late style since they seem to reflect a period of uncertainty, even crisis, towards Giottesque models. The figures of Saint Mary Magdalen and Saint Catherine are seen standing on each side of the Virgin. The coat of arms of the Segni family appears on the base of the throne.
(Room 4)

Painting of the 15th century

Three main factors characterized the 15th century in Florence: first, the city's experience of late Gothic culture; second, the cultural revival that intensified with the rise of Humanism and with the later Renaissance; and third, the spread of the Renaissance itself. The leading figures representing the International Gothic style in Florence were Lorenzo Ghiberti in sculpture, particularly the period of his first door for the Baptistery, and Lorenzo Monaco in painting. The influence of these artists was responsible for the creation of a Florentine late Gothic school that lasted throughout the first half of the 15th century. But in early 15th-century society other social forces sought new forms of expression and this led to profound changes that in Florence were introduced by Filippo Brunelleschi, Donatello and later Masaccio. In the midst of the numerous vicissitudes that made the Florentine environment of those years unique and distinguished the leading artists of the time, one painter emerged, Filippo Lippi, who succeeded in inventing a style that proved enormously successful and who propagated those artistic ideals which later became the common heritage of Florentine Renaissance society and which after 1460 witnessed the flourishing of important figures like Antonio del Pollaiolo, Verrocchio, Botticelli and Leonardo. This great period ended with the death of Lorenzo il Magnifico and the rise of Savonarola.

GENTILE DA FABRIANO
Adoration of the Magi
(1423)

The work, signed and dated in Gothic lettering, was executed for the Chapel of Palla di Noferi Strozzi in Santa Trinita during the artist's stay in Florence between 1422 and 1425. In the arches of this complex stage-like composition are Christ, the Annunciation, prophets and cherubs. Floral decorations grace the lateral pilasters, while the predella contains various religious scenes representing the Nativity, the Flight into Egypt and the Presentation in the Temple.
(Room 5/6)

MASACCIO and MASOLINO
Madonna and Child with Saint Anne and Five Angels
(1424-25)

This work, formerly in the church of Sant'Ambrogio, is mentioned by Vasari, though whether it formed part of a triptych or was independent is unclear. The distinction of hands proposed by Longhi, who attributed the Virgin and Child and the angel at top left to Masaccio and the whole of the rest of the painting to Masolino, has been accepted by most critics. The work certainly dates from after 1422, a period in which Masolino, before leaving Florence for Hungary, was obliged to find a companion to assist him in honouring work commitments.
(Room 7)

DOMENICO VENEZIANO
Santa Lucia dei Magnoli Altarpiece
(ca. 1440-50)

The work represents the enthroned Madonna and Child between Saints Francis, John the Baptist, Zenobius and Lucy. The predella, consisting of five panels showing episodes from the lives of the saints, is now housed in a dismembered state in the

museums of Washington, Cambridge and Berlin. The author is indicated by a written inscription at the bottom of the painting. The painting induces a sense of peaceful solemnity due to the symmetrical and regular composition in which the sense of space is rendered by an architectural structure several layers deep: the portico, a low exedra and the tops of the trees in the background.
(Room 7)

PIERO DELLA
FRANCESCA
**Portraits of the Duke
and Duchess of
Urbino**
(ca. 1465-70)

*Piero della Francesca
places these
medallion-style profile
portraits of Federigo
da Montefeltro and
his wife Battista
Sforza, boldly
standing out against
the Urbino landscape,
in mid-air, without
the traditional
support of a window
or curtain. The two
panels are also
painted on the back,
in an almost
miniaturistic style,
with allegorical
scenes illustrating the
virtues of the two
protagonists. In one,
the carriage of
Federigo and the four
Cardinal Virtues
advances theatrically
on a surface of false
rocks and against a
background of
faraway hills; the
other panel shows a
similar scene with
Battista Sforza and
the Theological
Virtues.*
(Room 7)

Filippo LIPPI
Madonna and Child with Angels
(ca. 1445)

*This work has always been considered one of the highest and most lyrical
expressions of Lippi's art. It is certainly a late composition, a distinct
foretaste of themes that would be developed by Botticelli, Pollaiolo and
Leonardo: the tension and incisiveness of the line, the typology of the
faces and the tender melancholy expressed by the persons portrayed. It
has been said that this work represents not a mother with her child, but
rather abstract figures absorbed in a vaster contemplation of private
thoughts and feelings.*
(Room 8)

BOTTICELLI
Primavera
(1482-83)

This painting, perhaps Botticelli's most popular and most exploited work, was seen by Vasari in the Villa di Castello of Cosimo I de' Medici. The name with which the canvas is universally known also derives from Vasari, although it is more likely that the artist, open to the learned advice of Poliziano and Marsilio Ficino, actually intended to represent the Realm of Venus. If this was the case the work should be interpreted in the following way: on the right Zephyrus pursues Flora, who, being possessed, scatters flowers over the world; Venus, in the centre, represents Humanitas, for whom the humanists of the Medicean circle reserved high tributes; the dancing Graces follow and on the far left Mercury disperses the clouds.
(Room 10/14)

BOTTICELLI
(1445-1510)

Painter. The Florentine artist Sandro Filipepi, known as Botticelli, trained as a painter in the workshops of Filippo Lippi and Verrocchio before opening one of his own that soon attracted the attention of contemporary high society. Protected by Lorenzo Il Magnifico and closely connected with the humanists of the Medici court, he devel-

oped a mysticism and philosophy that profoundly influenced all his art, distinguished by spiritual intensity and a deeply communicative chromatic brilliance. The allegories and classical myths of his early works were replaced in time with religious themes, previously heralded by the frescoes of the Sistine Chapel executed between 1481 and 1482 which marked the final act of Florentine Humanism.

BOTTICELLI
The Birth of Venus
(1484-86)

The subject probably derives from Ovid's Metamorphoses and Fasti - where the Hour (or Time) is described in the act of offering Venus her cloak - and therefore from all later humanistic literature. Although some see the painting as a representation of Venus landing on the shores of Sicily, blown by Zephyrus and Cloris, or at Portovenere, the residence of Simonetta Vespucci, it is more likely that the painting has a neo-Platonic cultural significance.
(Room 10/14)

PAOLO UCCELLO
Battle of San Romano
(1456)

The painting, signed at bottom left, represents an episode of the Battle of San Romano, possibly the unseating of Bernardino della Ciarda, a battle which the Florentines, under the command of Niccolò di Tolentino (portrayed in the Duomo by Andrea del Castagno) and Micheletto di Cotognola, won on 1 June 1432 against the Sienese. The painting forms part of a series of three works; the other two paintings, of a similar subject, are housed at the Louvre and the London National Gallery respectively. The painting, one of the most abstract plays of form and colour in Italian art, powerfully evokes the excitement and nightmare of medieval warfare - bristling lances, armoured, dehumanized warriors, clashes and entanglements - with unusual and indeed utterly unreal colours.
(Room 7)

Hugo VAN DER GOES
The Portinari Triptych: central panel
(1478)

*This large triptych is the most important work of the Flemish painter
Hugo van der Goes and is the basis for a reconstruction of the artist's
entire oeuvre. It was painted in Bruges and was commissioned to the
artist by Tommaso Portinari. The painting was intended for the high altar
of Sant'Egidio, the church of the Arcispedale of Santa Maria Nuova
founded in 1288 by the banker's ancestor Folco Portinari. The Adoration
of the Shepherds, dominated by the image of the Child radiantly lit in the
centre of the scene with the Madonna in Adoration, recalls the painting of
the same subject by Ghirlandaio now in the church of Santa Trinita and
reveals why the* Portinari Triptych *is rightfully considered unique in the
panorama of 15th-century Flemish painting.*
(Room 10/14)

LEONARDO
Annunciation
(1472-75)

This Annunciation was traditionally
attributed to Ghirlandaio and
subsequently to Verrocchio. The
prevailing view today is that it is
an early work by Leonardo, this
being suggested by the complexity
of the painting as a whole which
introduces many new elements.
The composition, for example, is
quite unsymmetrical. The angel
bowing down in front of the
Madonna is constructed along
bisecting diagonal lines; in this
way Leonardo avoids any
temptation to arrange the two
figures as complementary
structural forms.
(Room 15)

VERROCCHIO and LEONARDO
Baptism of Christ
(1472-75)

This is a fundamental work,
though one tormented by
historical vicissitudes. The stiffness
of the dove and the archaic hands
of God suggest that it may well
have entered Verrocchio's
workshop already prepared.
Subsequently entrusted to some
pupil, the painting was laid out in
a traditional way. When Leonardo
finally intervened he completely
upset the symmetry of the
composition.
(Room 15)

North European Painting

The first relations and exchanges between Germany and central and northern Italy date from the last decade of the 15th century. The protagonist of the first journey to Italy was Albrecht Dürer of Nuremberg, who later became the founder of the German Renaissance. The five paintings by Dürer at the Uffizi are important examples of this painter's art. The Uffizi has other paintings of considerable quality by Lukas Cranach the Elder, and has recently increased its already large group of German painters with the acquisition of two masterpieces by the leading exponent of the Danubian school, Albrecht Altdorfer. Also from the area of Germany is Hans Holbein the Younger, whose long residence in Basle gives him an intermediate position between the Rhine region, France and Italy. As regards Flanders and Holland, on the one hand the two regions were closely linked, on the other two clearly distinct artistic orientations were forming, this being due mainly to the tendency of Dutch painters to break away from their Flemish origins. After this, North European artists, especially those active in the wealthiest and most important city of the Low Countries, Antwerp, aspired to assimilate various fundamental principles established by Italian art and humanism such as the supremacy of the human figure. Towards the middle of the century Italian painting triumphed throughout the rest of Europe.

The Tribune and a detail of the Portrait of Lorenzo il Magnifico, *painted by Vasari after Lorenzo's death, and conserved here.*

The Tribune

The Tribune (Room 18) was built for Grand-duke Francesco I de' Medici by Bernardo Buontalenti and completed in 1589. It was furnished in such a way as to accommodate both sculptures and paintings of large and small dimensions. It was also intended as an anthology of the treasures of the Medici collections and a reflection of late 16th-century culture and artistic tastes at the end of the Renaissance. Over the centuries the treasures of the Tribune have been displayed in various ways. The present arrangement is a compromise between some aspects of the original layout and a selection of paintings, a somewhat debatable initiative since some of them have never before been displayed here. However, the choice is not entirely arbitrary since it does reflect the Trubune's original function. Indeed, the Tribune today presents a panorama of mature 16th-century art as it developed in Tuscany and Rome.

BRONZINO
Portrait of Eleonora of Toledo with her Son Giovanni
(1545)

The painting portrays the beautiful Eleonora of Toledo, daughter of the Viceroy of Naples and first wife of Cosimo I de' Medici (1539). The noblewoman is portrayed together with Giovanni, one of the eight children she bore for the Grand-duke. Sumptuous in the stiffness of the precious brocade dress, Eleonora rises before us with an almost architectural majesty. The outline is extremely fine and precise, and the modelling is essential, with no shadows or expressive lines, but only the impassive splendour of the lady's perfectly smooth, alabastrine flesh.
(Room 18)

ROSSO FIORENTINO
Musician Angel
(before 1530)

The musician angel is represented with a vivacity and movement that is particularly noticeable in the tawny hair, sprinkled with red and white, that seems to quiver in response to the music. Even the pointed wings stand up tautly like the strings of the mandolin.
(Room 18)

Painting of the 16th century

Giorgio Vasari was certainly right when he celebrated the 16th century as the one in which the figurative arts in Italy reached perfection. Italian art in fact achieved complete mastery both of style and human form. Beauty and intelligence were fused in what seemed an unrepeatable union. 16th-century art did not develop uniformly. On the contrary, few centuries have witnessed such a rapid succession of changes or the simultaneous existence of widely differing tendencies. Private and public space began to expand for political, economic and above all religious reasons, which had an enormous bearing on developments in the artistic world. In Florence, Rosso Fiorentino and Pontormo were the main exponents of the crisis of Classicism and of the tormented artistic vicissitudes in Italy in the first half of the 16th century. Mannerism was destined to become a national phenomenon with its centre of activity in Rome, where its greatest representative was certainly Michelangelo. After the middle of the century a new force, the Church of the Counter-Reformation, made its appearance with different historico-artistic objectives and the prevalence of ideals of abstract simplicity, even austerity. Vasari was one of the protagonists of this period in Florentine art. The end of the century witnessed the crisis of Mannerism, with two partly parallel developments: a return to the ordered, harmonious, reassuring world of early Florentine classicism, and the discovery of Venetian painting with its irresistible naturalistic charge.

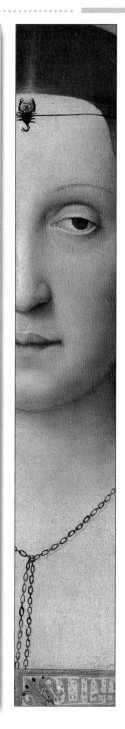

MICHELANGELO
Tondo Doni
(ca. 1506)

The Tondo Doni *(Holy Family with the Young Saint John) was executed on the occasion of the marriage of Agnolo Doni and Maddalena Strozzi, and is the only painting on wood which we know with certainty was by Michelangelo. It is a highly celebrated work, executed when Michelangelo had only just turned thirty but was already establishing himself as one of the greatest artists of his time. It is remarkable not only for the exceptional technical virtuosity, the thorough knowledge of anatomy, the variety and skill of the composition, but above all for the characterization and vigorous individuality of the figures.*
(Room 25)

RAPHAEL
Madonna of the Goldfinch
(1506)

In this work Raphael succeeds in producing a perfect synthesis of the broad, open composition of Leonardo and the compact, restricted one typical of Michelangelo. The pose and the gently shaded face of the Virgin are in fact in the style of Leonardo, whereas the central group is contained within a pyramid of Michelangiolesque stamp. The landscape shades off into blue transparencies with a horizontal line running the entire width of the painting.
(Room 26)

ANDREA DEL SARTO
Madonna of the Harpies
(1517)

The pedestal on which the Madonna is standing bears the date of the work and is decorated with the bizarre sculptures of two imaginary creatures, considered by some to be harpies, by others sphinxes. Some critics have seen in Saint Francis the artist's self-portrait and in the Madonna the face of his wife Lucrezia.
(Room 26)

TITIAN
Venus of Urbino
(1538)

This is an extremely fine composition. It invites us to dwell on more than just the warm, golden figure of this young woman with her cascading curls and the attractive, carefully studied movement of her arm. Observe the way the sheet has been painted, with masterful blends of colour, the small dog lazily curled up asleep, the amusing touch of the two maids rummaging in the chest, the world outside the window, and the malicious but at the same time ingenuous expression of the young Venus.
(Room 28)

Painting of the 17th and 18th century

The rooms in the Uffizi dedicated to the 17th and 18th centuries are an illustrious record of the participation of the last Medici rulers in the period of expansion of European collectionism which had started at the end of the 16th century. Although Cosimo III de' Medici was more interested in Dutch masters, it was he who acquired two valuable paintings by Rubens in 1686. The Uffizi also entered into possession of some important works by Van Dyck and by those artists who represented the poles of the revival that took place in Italy at the end of the 16th century: Caravaggio and Annibale Carracci. The interest of the Medici family in North European painting is amply reflected in the Florentine collections and concerns particularly various members of the grand-ducal family. In the first half of the 17th century this interest - which significantly regarded Cardinal Carlo and Cosimo II de' Medici, both sons of a north European woman, Christine of Lorraine - was to a large extent focused on landscapes. Another aspect of Medicean collectionism in keeping with the taste of the European princely courts of the late 17th century is represented by the series of small-format Dutch paintings and with interior scenes, bought by Cosimo III during his journeys to Holland, or coming from the Elector Palatine and his wife Anna Maria Ludovica. The room dedicated to the 18th century is a limited representation of what the Uffizi possesses of this century, a century which saw the end of the Medici dynasty and the reforming presence of the Lorraine family. Artistic activity was deeply affected by these events and was manifested in the falling off of the patronage of the last Medici and the emigration of numerous artists.

CARAVAGGIO
Bacchus
(late 16th C.)

This work, discovered and attributed relatively recently by Roberto Longhi, was of fundamental significance in the youthful activity of Caravaggio. As might be expected, the most varied interpretations of this painting have been advanced. According to Longhi, the ironic identification of Bacchus with "this sluggish youth of a Roman tavern" was controversially anti-classicist. Nonetheless, it is impossible to overlook in this work the references - ironic or otherwise - to classical antiquity both in the pose of the arm and in the Roman-style drapery.
(Room 16)

Jean Etienne LIOTARD
Marie Adelaide of France in Turkish Dress
(1753)

The theme of reading was typical of rococo artists. But Liotard excludes their tone of over-sweet sensuality, and instead, with clearer descriptiveness, accentuates the Oriental aspect. What strikes us about the figure engrossed in the reading of a French poetical work is the sense of an inner vitality.
(Room 45)

PONTE VECCHIO

This is the oldest bridge over the Arno river. It is mentioned in documents dating from before the year 1000 and may even have been built at the time of the Roman *Florentia*, with stone piers and a wooden roadway, to allow the crossing of the *Via Cassia*. This bridge, whatever its original nature, was destroyed by the flood of 1177 but subsequently rebuilt in stone and fortified with defence-towers. In 1333 it was again swept away by the raging waters of the Arno, an event recorded in the inscription under the sundial in the right terrace in the middle of the present bridge, rebuilt according to tradition by Taddeo Gaddi in 1345.

Benvenuto Cellini was chosen as the symbol of the bridge's new occupants and in 1900 the sculptor Raffaele Romanelli portrayed his likeness in the bronze bust of the decorative fountain. The Vasari Corridor passes over the porticos and workshops on the left side of the bridge.The three-arched bridge had porticos running along its sides under which were numerous shops, once occupied mainly by butchers. In the 16th century Ferdinando I de' Medici assigned the shops to goldsmiths, who over the years enlarged them by building characteristic little houses supported by brackets overhanging the river.

Ponte Vecchio with the Torre d'Arnolfo in the background.

ISTITUTO E MUSEO DI STORIA DELLA SCIENZA

The medieval Palazzo dei Giudici houses the glorious organism of the Institute and Museum of the History of Science where scientific instruments and objects from the antique collections of the Medicis and from various donations are reunited.It has two rich specialized libraries, restoration laboratories, storerooms, a planetarium, rooms for lectures and audio-visual presentations, etc. Among the most famous relics are Galileo's instruments and those used for the experiments carried out in the Accademia del Cimento; the armillary sphere, or planetary system according to Ptolemy; antique astrolabes; measuring instruments; galvanometers; batteries and various apparata that belonged to Alexander Volta; navigation instruments, etc.

The telescope and the lens used by Galileo to validate Copernicus' theory, which placed the Sun and not the Earth at the center of the known Universe.

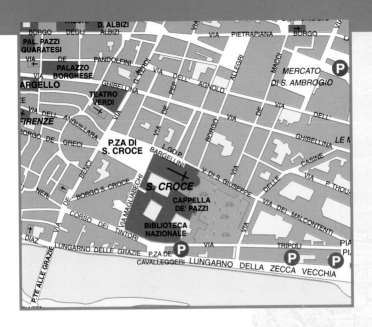

The Santa Croce District

This vast district, which includes the Palazzo Vecchio area, takes its name from the basilica of Santa Croce, the largest Franciscan church in the world. The church is an important stop for tourists, with its famous sepulchers and innumerable art masterpieces including Giotto's outstanding cycle of frescoes illustrating the Life of Saint Francis. The adjacent refectory building is now the home of Cimabue's splendid Crucifixion. The crucifix, now restored after having been damaged by the water and mud of 1966, has since become the symbol of the city devastated by the tragic flood. Piazza Santa Croce, on which the basilica stands, was at one time in history a forum for preachers and the site of public events, of which today there survive the Calcio Storico Fiorentino "soccer" games played in period costume. On the way back toward Piazza della Signoria, be sure to stop at the Museo Nazionale del Bargello, with its sculptures from the Florentine Renaissance and medieval times.

BASILICA AND CONVENT OF SANTA CROCE

The original church of Santa Croce was raised by the Franciscan Order of Minor Friars, who began the construction of a building of modest size in about 1228. 1n 1294 a new larger basilica started to be built around the early church, similar in practice to what happened for Santa Reparata. The monumental Gothic church was characterized by a sobriety and grandiosity that was perfectly in keeping with the Franciscan spirit that animated the friars of the adjoining convent. It is now firmly established that Santa Croce was built by Arnolfo di Cambio, the architect of a highly rational design entirely founded on modular calculus and on the geometrical figure of the square. Work continued and culminated in the enlargement carried out by Michelozzo in the first half of the 15th century, followed by the consecration of the basilica in 1443 in the presence of Pope Eugenius IV.

The outline of the basilica of Santa Croce.

A suggestive image of the facade of Santa Croce.

The **facade**, which remained unfinished, was completed in the 19th century by Nicolò Matas, who built it according to a tricuspidate Gothic model inspired by designs by Cronaca. The campanile was also built in the 19th century on a design by Gaetano Baccani.

The **convent** is situated next to the right flank of the church and is arranged around two cloisters, the first of which is completed by one of the masterpieces of Florentine Renaissance architecture, the **Pazzi Chapel**, designed by Brunelleschi. The whole complex, including the precious works contained in it, was heavily damaged in the flood of 1966, but was very quickly restored to its original beauty.

Interior - The church's monumental interior clearly reveals the Gothic elements of Arnolfo di Cambio's building which is divided into a nave and two side aisles by octagonal pilasters in pietra forte supporting high pointed arches. The nave, with a gallery running along its entire length supported by brackets and accompanied by pointed arched windows, is covered by a painted trussed roof and embellished by a magnificent 15th-century *pulpit*, the work of Benedetto da Maiano. The transept, whose T-shape is grafted onto the end of the nave and aisles, is characterized at its centre by the so-called *Cappella Maggiore*, which acts as an apse and is entered through an enormous pointed arch in line with the central nave. Departing from the Cappella Maggiore the two arms of the transept are lined with numerous noblemen's chapels containing many precious works.

The interior of the basilica and the Cappella Maggiore.

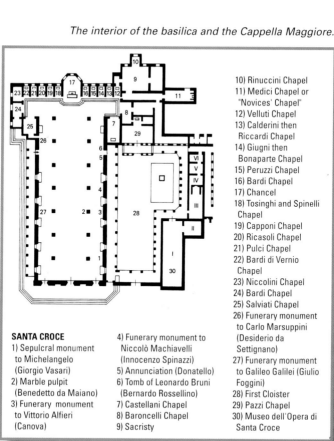

10) Rinuccini Chapel
11) Medici Chapel or "Novices' Chapel"
12) Velluti Chapel
13) Calderini then Riccardi Chapel
14) Giugni then Bonaparte Chapel
15) Peruzzi Chapel
16) Bardi Chapel
17) Chancel
18) Tosinghi and Spinelli Chapel
19) Capponi Chapel
20) Ricasoli Chapel
21) Pulci Chapel
22) Bardi di Vernio Chapel
23) Niccolini Chapel
24) Bardi Chapel
25) Salviati Chapel
26) Funerary monument to Carlo Marsuppini (Desiderio da Settignano)
27) Funerary monument to Galileo Galilei (Giulio Foggini)
28) First Cloister
29) Pazzi Chapel
30) Museo dell'Opera di Santa Croce

SANTA CROCE
1) Sepulcral monument to Michelangelo (Giorgio Vasari)
2) Marble pulpit (Benedetto da Maiano)
3) Funerary monument to Vittorio Alfieri (Canova)
4) Funerary monument to Niccolò Machiavelli (Innocenzo Spinazzi)
5) Annunciation (Donatello)
6) Tomb of Leonardo Bruni (Bernardo Rossellino)
7) Castellani Chapel
8) Baroncelli Chapel
9) Sacristy

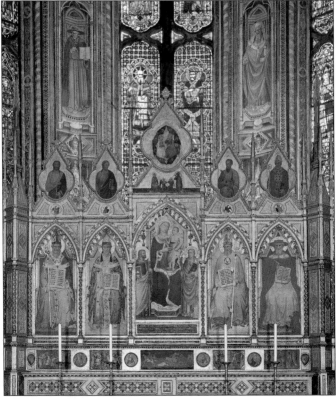

Giorgio VASARI
**Sepulchral monument
to Michelangelo**
(1570)

The monument was designed by
Vasari to celebrate the great
master in his threefold guise as
painter, sculptor and architect
through the allegorical figures
seated at the base of the
sarcophagus representing the
three arts. Above the bust of
Michelangelo is a fresco of the
Pietà, a subject dear to the artist.

DONATELLO
Annunciation
(1435)

The work, which Donatello executed
together with Michelozzo, is
perhaps one of the greatest
masterpieces of the Florentine
Renaissance. The scene of the
Annunciation to Mary is magisterially
evoked in this small tabernacle in
gilded pietra serena through the
expression of the faces and
postures of the Virgin and the
Archangel. The dramatic twisting of
the body of Mary, shown standing,
revealed by the elaborate drapery,
expresses her surprise at the
appearance of the angel, who gently
conveys to her the glad tidings. The tabernacle is inserted into an
elegant structure adorned with carvings and surmounted by small
angels in terracotta.

BENEDETTO DA MAIANO
Pulpit
(1472-76)

The five bas-reliefs which make up this fine octagonal marble pulpit are dedicated, like many other works adorning Santa Croce, to the life and works of St Francis. The scenes illustrate the salient moments of the Franciscan mission, from the Approval of the Rule to the Mission before the Sultan, and of the earthly existence of the saint, who is portrayed receiving the Stigmata. Below the marble panels five small statues portraying the Virtues occupy the niches created between the supporting brackets.

Giulio FOGGINI
Funerary monument to Galileo Galilei
(1574-1642)

The tomb of the great astronomer, who is portrayed in the bust by Giovan Battista and Vincenzo Foggini, is surrounded by two allegorical figures representing Astronomy and Geometry, the latter an 18th-century work by Girolamo Ticciati.

Taddeo GADDI
Stories of Mary
(1332-38)
Baroncelli Chapel

Taddeo Gaddi was the faithful pupil and most important follower of Giotto. From him he drew the masterful choice of colours and the exaltation of the human figure, whose centrality is reaffirmed in the episodes from the life of the Virgin frescoed in the Baroncelli Chapel. The events represented are, from top to bottom and from left to right, *the* Expulsion from the Temple of St Joachim, *the elderly father of Mary, the* Annunciation of the Angel to Joachim, *the* Meeting with St Anne at the Gate of Jerusalem, *the* Birth of Mary, *the* Presentation in the Temple *and the* Marriage of the Virgin.

The Cappella Baroncelli.

At the head of the transept, next to the door leading into the Sacristy, is the **Baroncelli Chapel,** frescoed by Taddeo Gaddi with *Stories of Mary* and decorated with the *Coronation of the Virgin*, a polyptych produced by Giotto's *bottega*.
Giotto painted the frescoes with the *Stories of St Francis of Assisi* which adorn the **Bardi Chapel**, an expression of the most mature art of the greatest 14th-century painter. The original Gothic structure was altered by Vasari, who in 1560 made radical modifications especially in the side aisles and demolished works of considerable value like the choir.
In the right side aisle the splendid 15th-century aedicule sculpted by Donatello representing the *Annunciation* was saved. The church's old function as a burial-place of the most important members of Florentine noble families, begun in the 14th century, was continued in later centuries and made Santa Croce a veritable monument to the glories of the past.

Anonymous artist
St Francis and twenty Stories of his life
(13th C.)
Bardi Chapel

This fine 13th-century painting once attributed to Barone Berlinghieri, in which Byzantine influences are clearly discernible, was executed in the first half of the 13th century by an unknown Florentine artist.
Around the figure of the saint are the most important episodes of his life.

The Cappella Bardi.

Among the many tombs that characterize the building there are in fact those of some of the greatest artistic geniuses of Italian art, literature and science. As well as the *cenotaph of Dante* and the *tombs of Foscolo* and *Alfieri* there is also the *Tomb monument to Michelangelo* and the *Funerary monument to Galileo Galilei.*
The tall, airy **Cappella Maggiore** of Santa Croce, which is graced by three splendid high Gothic stained-glass windows, was completely frescoed around 1380 by Agnolo Gaddi, who illustrated on the walls the *Legend of the Holy Cross,* a popular theme in the 14th-century iconographical tradition. The pilasters were instead decorated with figures of *Saints* inside Gothic niches, which are taken up in the stained-glass windows, also designed by Gaddi. The vault, again by the master, is frescoed with figures of the *Redeemer,* the *Evangelists* and *St Francis.* Above the altar is a large polyptych composed in the 19th century representing the *Madonna with Saints and Fathers of the Church* by various 14th-century artists, and the majestic *Crucifix* by the so-called Master of Figline, a fine example of the 14th-century Giottesque school.

Sacristy - A long corridor, built according to a design by Michelozzo and lit by splendid three-arched Gothic windows, leads to the Sacristy, a large 14th-century room with a trussed roof and walls frescoed with paintings dating from the first half of the 14th century. Particularly noteworthy are the frescoes on the right wall representing a superb *Crucifixion* in the centre, the work of Taddeo Gaddi, with, at the sides, the *Ascent to Calvary*, attributed to Spinello Aretino, and the *Resurrection* by Niccolò Gerini, one of whose pupils is attributed with the *Ascension* surmounting the other three works. The show-cases arranged along the perimeter of the room contain codexes and sacred furnishings belonging to various periods. Adjoining the Sacristy is also the 14th-century **Rinuccini Chapel,** complete with a wrought-iron railing dated 1371 and embellished with a fine polyptych representing a *Madonna and Child with Saints* and frescoes whose compositional schemes recall

GIOTTO
(1267-1337)

Passing from his native Mugello to the Florentine school of Cimabue, and from here to an important period in Rome, Giotto brought to painting a current of profound renewal. The painted buildings of the backgrounds and the plastic emphasis of the figures in the Stories of St Francis in the Upper Basilica of Assisi betray in fact clear Cosmatesque influences and a certain hint of the art of Arnolfo di Cambio. Characteristics that would reappear, filtered by a more austere artistic maturity, in the frescoes of the Arena Chapel in Padua. Many of his works are to be found in Florence, where in 1334 Giotto was appointed chief architect of the Opera del Duomo.

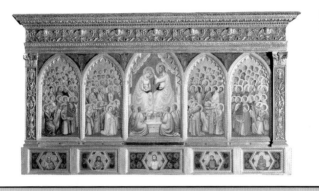

Above, the Coronation of the Virgin, *a polyptych produced by Giotto's* bottega, *in the Cappella Baroncelli.*

On the facing page, The Death of Saint Francis *frescoed by Giotto.*

the works of Taddeo Gaddi and represent episodes of the *Stories of Mary Magdalen* and *Stories of Mary.*

Refectory - Together with other rooms forming part of the old Franciscan convent, the Refectory houses the **Museo dell'Opera di Santa Croce**, which contains some of the most important pictorial works of the Florentine Duecento, primarily the monumental *Crucifix* by Cimabue. The large hall, originally used by the monks for eating their meals in contemplation and prayer, is a rectangular structure with a trussed roof lit by high Gothic mullioned windows framed by black and white bands. The end wall is entirely frescoed with six scenes painted by Taddeo Gaddi: among these the *Last Supper,* an iconographical theme often used in the decoration of refectories, extends at the bottom below the colossal *Tree of the Cross,* decorated with busts of *Prophets,* full-length figures of *Saints,* including St Francis, and the *Pious Women* adoring the Crucifix.

93

The sacristy with the Cappella Rinuccini.

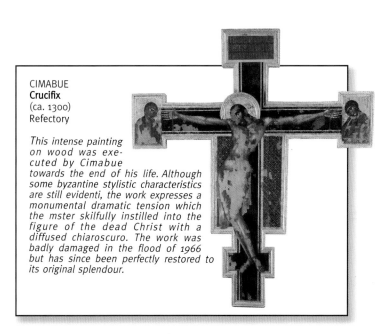

CIMABUE
Crucifix
(ca. 1300)
Refectory

This intense painting on wood was executed by Cimabue towards the end of his life. Although some byzantine stylistic characteristics are still evidenti, the work expresses a monumental dramatic tension which the mster skilfully instilled into the figure of the dead Christ with a diffused chiaroscuro. The work was badly damaged in the flood of 1966 but has since been perfectly restored to its original splendour.

PAZZI CHAPEL

At the end of the first cloister of the convent of Santa Croce stands one of the most original works of that genius of Renaissance architecture, Filippo Brunelleschi. This is the chapel which the artist began building in 1443 for Andrea de' Pazzi, a member of one of the most illustrious Florentine families, but which he never saw finished. He succeeded in fact in constructing the graceful pronaos characterized by six Corinthian columns in pietra serena, but died before the completion of the facade. The mastery of the Florentine architect is evident, however, in the superb **interior.**

Rectangular in plan, surmounted by a cupola with a low cylindrical drum and truncated cone roof, it is characterized by harmonious ribs and pilaster strips in pietra serena which stand out against the white of the walls and vaults. Other decorative elements are the *Della Robbia polychrome terracottas* adorning the pendentives of the cupola and the walls. The former, representing the four Evangelists, were probably made according to a design by Brunelleschi, whereas the wall roundels in white glaze on a light-blue background, representing the Apostles, are by Luca Della Robbia.

The Cappella de' Pazzi and two Della Robbia roundels in its interior.

Cappella de' Pazzi: interior.

CASA BUONARROTI

In Via Ghibellina, a short distance from the basilica of Santa Croce, is the house which Michelangelo bought for his nephew Leonardo, and which the latter's son, Michelangelo the Younger, a brilliant man of letters, had decorated in the 17th century with scenes of the life of his illustrious great-uncle.

In the middle of the 19th century, the last member of the Michelangelo family left the house to the Florence city council which turned it into a museum. It contains, in addition to copies of some of Michelangelo's compositions and 16th- and 17th-century works, numerous preliminary drawings and sketches which the artist produced in the course of his life, starting from the earliest years of his long career as a painter and sculptor, but also as an architect, as is revealed by the interesting *Study for the facade of San Lorenzo*. The seed of another monumental work by Michelangelo is the *Study for the Last Judgement*, which the master executed in the Sistine Chapel in Rome. Other red-ochre and pencil drawings depict mighty human figures and Titanic bodies, such as the *Study of a Nude*, or dramatic female creatures, like *Cleopatra*, but also religious subjects, like the intense *Madonna and Child*.

Some of the sketches preserved in Casa Buonarroti.

LOGGIA DEL PESCE

The loggia was built by Vasari in 1567. It originally stood in the area of the Mercato Vecchio, present-day Piazza della Repubblica, but was removed from this area during the demolition and clearance of the old city centre. Disassembled in its essential parts, the loggia was rebuilt in *Piazza dei Ciompi*, where there is now a delightful little Flea Market, a real treasure-trove for antique enthusiasts interested in finding valuable objects at reasonable prices.

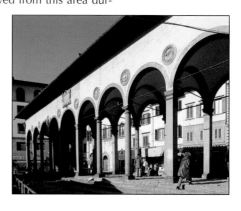

BIBLIOTECA NAZIONALE CENTRALE

An Italian institution of considerable prestige, the Biblioteca Nazionale Centrale houses extremely precious collections of documents, letters, manuscripts, codexes, incunabula, engravings, miniatures, geographical maps and some of the rarest printed editions in the world. In 1885, by royal decree, the Library received a copy of every published work in Italy. The more than 4 million volumes now present are the fruit of numerous acquisitions that have greatly enlarged the original collection of about 30,000 works, the so-called Biblioteca Magliabechiana, created by the bequest of Antonio Magliabechi, the librarian of Cosimo III de' Medici. The Magliabechiana was opened to the public in 1747 and was soon joined by the Biblioteca Lotaringia and the Biblioteca Palatina, founded by the Lorraine grand-dukes.

Numerous other possessions belonging to the most illustrious families and most important Florentine convents were subsequently acquired until in 1861 the various collections were combined to form the present National Library. To house it the large building along the banks of the Arno was erected between 1911 and 1935.

In 1966 the Library's collections suffered heavy damage in the ruinous flooding of the river Arno, but thanks to the great contribution of many people they have now been almost completely repaired.

DANTE'S HOUSE

This interesting institution, celebrating one of the most famous of all Florentine glories, almost has the air of wanting to make amends for the grave injustice suffered almost seven centuries ago by the great poet who died in exile, never to return again to his native city. As a matter of fact, not even the house was really his. The dwellings of the Alighieri family also fell victim to the bitter feuds between the White and Black Guelf factions and was razed to the ground. The building today called "Dante's House", which is noteworthy for its reconstruction of the rooms, does however fulfil its function of recalling and celebrating Dante and attracts many visitors as well as housing numerous cultural events.

The Biblioteca Nazionale Centrale;
Dante in the panel by Domenico di
Michelino in the Duomo;
the entrance to the Casa di Dante.

PALAZZO DEL BARGELLO

The Bargello was, after Palazzo Vecchio, the second most important public building of medieval Florence, though since it was built in 1255 it predated the latter by almost half a century. It was originally built as the headquarters of the Captain of the People. It stood next to the sturdy, elegant tower of the Bonizzi family, the so-called 'Torre Volognana', named after Geri da Volognano, the Ghibelline who was imprisoned there in 1267. The oldest part of the palace was built on the design of two Dominican friars, Sisto and Ristoro, as a sort of rectangular fortress with two austere main facades, those facing west and south, divided horizontally into three fasciae by two thin cornices. The central storey is characterized by a row of two-arched bays above which runs a row of smaller simple windows.

In the facade overlooking Piazza San Firenze the second cornice is interrupted by a large Gothic two-arched bay, inserted in 1345 at the time work was being carried out to enlarge the palace at the back, whose fronts are characterized instead by taller two-arched

windows and a row of lobed windows above. At the top of the building is an overhanging crenellation supported by Gothic arches. The palace did not always house the same public offices. In 1261 it became the seat of the Podestà; from 1502 it housed the Council of Justice or Tribunale della Ruota, and later still, in 1574, the Captain of Justice, that is, the city police chief, also known as the Bargello, from *bargildus*, an office existing in the Carolingian period. At the present time this magnificent palace houses the Museo Nazionale del Bargello, arranged on three floors of the building around a delightful **courtyard.**

MUSEO NAZIONALE DEL BARGELLO

The Ticket Office leads into a picturesque courtyard, enclosed on three sides by a powerful colonnade supported by octagonal pilasters, whose walls are literally covered with the coats of arms of the **Podestà**, the **Quarters**, the **Districts** and the **Gonfalons**, most of them reconstructions dating from the last century. Along the west wall is the **monumental staircase** designed by Neri di Fioravante (1345-1367), at whose base is a stone *Marzocco lion*, the symbol of Florence. At the top is the **loggia** (1319), an architectural jewel attributed to Tone di Giovanni. In the courtyard, under the colonnade, is the bronze *Cannon of St Paul*.

On the ground floor, on the same side as the staircase, is the **Room of Michelangelo and 16th-century Sculpture**, where there are various works by the artist including the statues of *Bacchus, Brutus, Apollo* or *David*, and the *Pitti Madonna*, together with the *Bacchus* by Sansovino, the *Bust of Cosimo I* by Baccio Bandinelli, numerous small bronzes made by Cellini for the *Perseus* group (*Hermes, Athena, Zeus* and the bas-relief with *Perseus Freeing Andromeda*), the statue of *Hermes* by Giambologna (whose curious bronze *Peacock* is also on display) and one of Cellini's

Bargello. Above, Giambologna's bronze Peacock *(1567) and the monumental staircase in the inner courtyard.*

great masterpieces, the *Bust of Cosimo I*. On the other side of the courtyard is the **Room of Medieval Sculpture**, which contains sculptures, reliefs and architectural elements from religious buildings and monuments of the Florentine state. The five-arched loggia of the balcony above leads to the first-floor rooms, notable among them the **Room of Donatello or 'Udienza'.** Here we can admire two precious terracottas by Luca della Robbia: the *Madonna and Child with Two Angels* and the *Madonna of the Rosegarden,* together with the celebrated *David* by Donatello, the *Bust of Niccolò da Uzzano*, the *Attis* or Eros by the same artist and the two panels representing the *Sacrifice of Isaac*, one executed by Ghiberti and the other by Brunelleschi for the competition held in 1401 for the door of the Baptistery. Numerous rooms are dedicated to the Lesser Arts, including the **Carrand Room**, from the name of the French antique-dealer who donated his collection to the museum at the end of the 19th century, and the **Room of the Maiolicas**, which houses numerous precious objects of various periods and provenance. To the east of the Carrand Room, lastly, the **Cappella del Podestà** still houses precious wall frescoes representing *Paradise* and *Hell*. Among the most interesting rooms of the second floor is the one dedicated to **Giovanni Della Robbia,** where, among other terracottas, is the highly evocative *Pietà*.

The head of Saint Paul decorates the bronze cannon (1638) by Cosimo Cenni in the inner portico (below).

MICHELANGELO
David or Apollo
(1530-32)

A marble statue sculpted by Michelangelo for Baccio Valori, this classical style youth represents one of the artist's loftiest achievements and belongs to the period in which he worked on the statues of the Tombs of Lorenzo and Giuliano for the Medici Chapels. For a long time the work remained in the rooms of Cosimo I de' Medici before being moved to the amphitheatre of the Boboli Gardens. In 1824 it was transferred to the Uffizi and since 1871 has been housed in the Bargello.

SANSOVINO
Bacchus
(1520)

The work dates from the last years of the artist's Florentine period, before his departure for Rome. Although inspired by classical models, this extremely harmonious nude is the result of a meticulous study of anatomical detail. For a long time the work was kept in Palazzo Vecchio, then at the Uffizi, where it was damaged in the fire of 1762, before finally being moved to the Bargello. As in Michelangelo's Bacchus, here too a little satyr is trying to bite the bunches of grapes which the young god is holding in his hand.

MICHELANGELO
Bacchus
(1497-99)

This was the first large-scale free-standing statue executed by Michelangelo. Commissioned by the banker Jacopo Galli and made in Rome, the work bears witness to the influence on the artist of classical sculpture.

Benvenuto CELLINI
Mercury
(mid-16th C.)

*The dynamism and expressive tension of the god's
body have been masterfully rendered by the artist
through the springy movement of the limbs and the
body's agile posture. This work forms part of the
Perseus group.*

Benvenuto CELLINI
Athena (mid-16th C.)

*Athena too supported Perseus in his
heroic deed by giving him a shield.
For this reason Cellini wanted the
goddess of wisdom also to be
present in the sculpture dedicated
to the hero.*

BENVENUTO CELLINI
Model for the Perseus
(mid-16th C.)

*This small bronze statue
standing on a base with a pink
marble column was probably the model for
the casting of the final statue and was later given
as a gift to Grand-duchess Eleonora of Toledo.
Traces of gilding would confirm that for some time it
was used as the centre of a table fountain for wine.*

MICHELANGELO
Pitti Madonna
(1504-08)

*More or less contemporary with the David
and executed for Bartolomeo Pitti, this
marble relief represents the figures of the
Madonna, the Child and the young St John
and reveals the influence of the chiaroscuro
technique of Leonardo da Vinci. The three
figures are inserted into the roundel with
wonderful harmony and the head of the
Virgin, which exceeds the limits of the tondo,
confers to the work a dynamism and
monumentality that are also found in the slightly earlier 'Tondo Doni'
of the Uffizi.*

MICHELANGELO
Brutus
(ca. 1540)

A marble bust executed for Cardinal Ridolfi after the assassination of Lorenzino de' Medici, who in turn had murdered the detested Duke Alessandro de' Medici, the oppressor of Florentine liberties. Because Michelangelo left the work unfinished owing to his own doubts about the political tyrannicide, the drapery was completed by Tiberio Calcagni.

Benvenuto CELLINI
Bust of Cosimo I
(1545-47 and 1555-57)

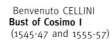

In his autobiography Cellini mentioned the solemn bust as his first large-scale casting in bronze. In actual fact at first only the head was cast, the bust being added later between 1555 and 1557. Placed at the entrance of the fortress of Portoferraio, which Cosimo I de' Medici had had built on the island of Elba in 1548, the work returned to Florence in 1781 and was housed first at the Uffizi and subsequently at the Bargello.

LUCA DELLA ROBBIA
Madonna and Child with Two Angels
(1450)

This splendid lunette in enamelled terracotta has colours typical of Luca della Robbia, white and pale blue, enriched by an arched cornice with ovuli and garlands of daisies and calendula. The lilies held by the angels are symbols of the Immaculate Conception.

BADIA FIORENTINA

An ancient tradition relates that a couple of decades before the year 1000 Count Ugo of Tuscany founded seven abbeys in the Florence area, including one within the city walls called the Badia Fiorentina where he himself was later buried. In actual fact the abbey was founded by Ugo's mother, Willa, who laid the first stone in 978. The building was subsequently enlarged and modified by Arnolfo di Cambio according to the canons of Cistercian architecture in 1282. Thirty years later, in 1310, work was started on the construction of the **bell-tower**, a soaring hexagonal structure built on a square plan. The two lower orders are characterized by Romanesque-style windows while the upper two, added in 1330, are in the Gothic style with elegant two-arched bays. At the top of the tower a slender spire rises in the middle of six triangular tympanums. In 1627 the Arnolfian church was radically modified by Matteo Segaloni, who even changed its orientation by converting the early building into the transept of the present church. The complex also comprises the cloister of the old monastery, the so-called *Chiostro degli Aranci*, and the 16th-century *Cappella Pandolfini*. The entrance is directly opposite the Palazzo del Bargello and was once reached by a double flight of steps.

The profile of the soaring bell tower of the Badia Fiorentina facing the squared-off, crenelated "Volognana Tower" of the Bargello.

ORSANMICHELE

There is an interesting story behind this church's unusual name. It was not a religious building originally, but a loggia for the grain market, built on a design by Arnolfo di Cambio in 1290 within the boundary of the garden ('orto') attached to the old monastery of San Michele (hence the name).

The loggia was destroyed by a fire in 1304 and replaced thirty-three years later by a larger construction with upper-floor granaries built by Francesco Talenti, Neri di Fioravanti and Neri di Cione. The granaries were reached by means of a stairway built inside one of the outer pillars, while the stored grain was poured down through shutes and emerged through holes in some of the pillars on the floor below.

In 1380 the arches running round the outside of the loggia, already decorated with magnificent Gothic three-arched bays, were closed up so that the building could be used as a church.

A lovely view from above of Orsanmichele with the dome of the Cappella dei Principi in the background.

In the following century, at the instigation of the various city guilds, elegant **niches** were made in the outer pilasters to house **statues** of the patron saints of these corporations. Some are particularly fine works, including the statue of *Saint James*, protector of the 'Pellicciai' (furriers), probably the work of Niccolò Lamberti, and the bronze statue of *Saint Stephen*, protector of the 'Lanaiuoli' (wool manufacturers and clothiers), made by Lorenzo Ghiberti in 1428. When no longer used as a granary, the two upper floors, built in pietra forte and decorated with airy two-arched marble windows, were used first as a Notary's Archive and later as the seat of the Dante Society.

The early use of this unusual building as a loggia for the grain market is particularly evident in the rectangular **interior**, which is divided into two aisles by quadrangular pilasters supporting high cross vaults. Some of the pilasters still have the holes through which the grain, stored on the upper floors, was poured. In addition to the frescoes on the vaults and pilasters, and various paintings, the interior is embellished by the votive altar dedicated to Saint Anne in the left aisle, and by the **Tabernacle by Orcagna** in the right aisle.

One of the elegant aediculae that decorate the exterior of Orsanmichele.

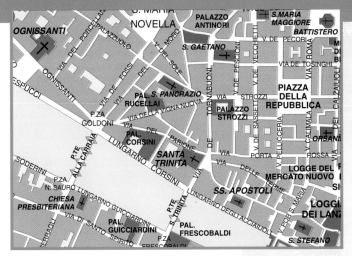

Santa Trinita, Via Tornabuoni, and the Loggia del Mercato Nuovo

*F*rom the historical arches of Ponte Santa Trinita we descend into one of the world's most luxurious, elegant streets, the ancient Via Tornabuoni. This area was at the heart of Julius Caesar's Florentia—although it is a bit difficult to imagine, today, that this exclusive shopping area populated by famous-name boutiques hides the remains of the Roman circle of walls. The term "historical center" in fact embraces the area between Via Tornabuoni and Santa Croce—where a "Via delle Terme" and a "Via del Campidoglio" have survived the centuries—and recalls the splendors of that first Florence, as does the 19th-century development work that recreated, in Piazza della Repubblica, the open space that was the forum in Roman times. Around and along Via Tornabuoni are some of the

city's most sumptuous historical homes, from the refined Palazzo Rucellai designed by Alberti to the grandiose Palazzo Strozzi by Benedetto da Maiano, now the site of many important exhibits. Of course, we recommend a stop at the Loggia del Mercato Nuovo, an open-air market where you'll find souvenirs and typically Florentine products in straw and leather.

PIAZZA DELLA REPUBBLICA

The present-day Piazza della Repubblica (formerly *Piazza Vittorio Emanuele II*) was once the heart of medieval Florence, and even earlier of Roman Florence. This was originally the site of the Forum, the centre of the city's public and commercial life, where many centuries later the **Mercato Vecchio** established itself, conserving the mercantile vocation of the old Roman site. Around it was the Jewish quarter, or **Ghetto**, full of charming streets and alleys which numerous painters, including Telemaco Signorini, reproduced in drawings and canvases towards the end of the 19th century, shortly before it finally disappeared.

LOGGIA DEL MERCATO NUOVO

Built in the middle of the 16th century by Giovan Battista Del Tasso, the loggia, which was originally a meeting-place and bargaining-ground for merchants of precious fabrics and gold, today houses a colourful market of Florentine handicrafts. The square loggia has four arches on each side supported by columns and pilasters. The corner pilasters are decorated with niches containing 19th-century statues representing important characters in the historical and cultural life of Florence. On the pavement, in the centre, is a marble disc on which, in the Middle Ages, the 'Carroccio' was placed before its departure for the battlefield and where, in times of peace, the backsides of bankrupt traders were beaten as a corporal punishment for financial offences.

Piazza della Repubblica.

The Loggia del Mercato Nuovo, the Boar of the fountain affectionately known as "il Porcellino" and, bottom, Palazzo Rucellai.

Fontana del Porcellino - In 1612, along the southern side of the loggia, the so-called Fontana del Porcellino was placed, a bronze work by Pietro Tacca inspired by an ancient marble original now at the Uffizi, in which travellers traditionally throw a coin to propitiate their return to Florence.

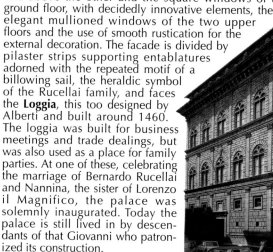

PALAZZO RUCELLAI

The palace was built around the middle of the 15th century by Bernardo Rossellino as the residence of Giovanni Rucellai, a wealthy businessman and Florentine patron, who entrusted its design to Leon Battista Alberti.

The building which Alberti had conceived according to the theoretical principles of the Renaissance is the mature expression of the most harmonious union of motifs drawn from Roman antiquity, such as the division of the facade into three architectural orders one above the other and the square windows of the ground floor, with decidedly innovative elements, the elegant mullioned windows of the two upper floors and the use of smooth rustication for the external decoration. The facade is divided by pilaster strips supporting entablatures adorned with the repeated motif of a billowing sail, the heraldic symbol of the Rucellai family, and faces the **Loggia**, this too designed by Alberti and built around 1460. The loggia was built for business meetings and trade dealings, but was also used as a place for family parties. At one of these, celebrating the marriage of Bernardo Rucellai and Nannina, the sister of Lorenzo il Magnifico, the palace was solemnly inaugurated. Today the palace is still lived in by descendants of that Giovanni who patronized its construction.

PONTE SANTA TRINITA

In 1252 it was decided to build a wooden foot-bridge, not far from Ponte Vecchio, joining the two banks of the Arno on which medieval Florence was developing. The structure proved to be inadequate against the impetuous floodwaters of the river, which swept it away in 1333. About ten years later the reconstruction of the bridge, this time in stone, was entrusted to the same builder of the much more solid Ponte Vecchio, Taddeo Gaddi. His five-arched structure resisted for more than two centuries, but it too eventually succumbed to the waters of the Arno in 1557.

These statues, representing the **Four Seasons**, were added in 1608 on the occasion of the marriage of Cosimo II de' Medici and Maria Maddalena of Austria. Destroyed during the Second World War, the bridge was rebuilt in its original form after the recovery of materials that had fallen into the river.

A new bridge was planned, for which the city authorities summoned Bartolomeo Ammannati, who worked on its construction from 1567 to 1570, making a strong, elegant structure with three polycentric arches resting on massive acute-angled piers. Ammannati's bridge, the design of which Vasari submitted to Michelangelo for approval, had oval arches whose keystones were concealed by marble scrolls. It did not include the statues which decorate the two ends of the bridge.

Ponte Santa Trinita with Ponte Vecchio in the background.

Column of Justice - In front of the church of Santa Trinita, in the centre of the square of the same name, stands the imposing monolithic porphyry column surmounted by a statue representing *Justice*, the work of Francesco Ferrucci, otherwise known as Tadda, which celebrates an important event in the history of the Florentine state. The column, coming from the Baths of Caracalla in Rome and donated by Pope Pius IV to Cosimo de' Medici in 1560, was in fact placed in Piazza Santa Trinita to commemorate Cosimo's victory over the rebels led by Filippo Strozzi at Montemurlo on 2 August 1537. The symbolic value of the statue, placed at the top of the column in 1581, reinforces what was represented by the position of the monument itself, placed as a reference-point at the crossing of two important main roads in the urban layout of Renaissance Florence: one, lined with handsome noble residences, linking *Via Tornabuoni* to *Via Maggio*, in Oltrarno, by way of Ponte Santa Trinita, the other leading along *Via delle Terme* to Palazzo Vecchio, whose tower is clearly visible from the base of the column.

CHURCH OF SANTA TRINITA

The church was built as an oratory for the Vallombrosan Order in the second half of the 11th century, and by 1258, when it was completely remodelled in the Gothic style, was known by the name of *Santa Maria dello Spasimo*. The name of the architect who worked this innovative transformation is unknown, although the **facade**, built between 1593 and 1594 in a Mannerist style already heralding the Baroque, is certainly the work of Bernardo Buontalenti. The lower part of the facade is divided by pilaster strips with modified Corinthian capitals, while in the upper part it ends in a single bay surmounted by a tympanum, in which there is a round window. Over the central door a high relief representing the *Holy Trinity*, the work of Giovanni Caccini, interrupts the symmetrical play of the windows above the side doors. Santa Trinita is the first church in Florence in which Gothic structural innovations appear, these being evident in the interior: a Latin cross plan, clustered pilasters, pointed arches and cross vaults, elements and structures that would be superbly taken up two decades after their introduction in the building of Santa Maria Novella.

GHIRLANDAIO
Adoration of the Shepherds
(1485)
Sassetti Chapel

The work shows the peculiar union of typically Flemish stylistic characteristics and classical elements drawn from Humanistic culture and the rediscovery of Roman antiquities on which it was based. These are present in the marble arch which serves as a manger, in the Corinthian pilasters supporting the roof of the barn and in the triumphal arch under which the procession of people coming to adore the Child is passing. Elements of Flemish inspiration are evident in the figures of the shepherds and the background landscape, which are reminiscent of those in the Portinari Triptych *by Hugo van der Goes at the Uffizi.*

The **interior** of Santa Trinita contains important works by great Tuscan masters like Lorenzo Monaco and Domenico Ghirlandaio, the latter being the author of the 15th-century frescoes of the **Sassetti Chapel**, which also contains the celebrated *Adoration of the Shepherds* by the same artist. Adjoining the church was the **convent of Santa Trinita**, whose rooms now house the Teacher Training Faculty.

PALAZZO ANTINORI

The construction of the palace, probably on a design by Giuliano da Maiano, was commissioned in 1461 by Giovanni Boni, a businessman and member of the Moneychangers' Guild. Unfortunately, he never saw the building finished since he died before the conclusion of the work in 1469. A few years later the palace was sold by Giovanni's father to Lorenzo il Magnifico, who in turn sold it to the Martelli family. At the beginning of the 16th century it finally came into the possession of the Antinori, a prestigious Florentine family whose name it now bears.

The palace, consisting of three storeys built around an elegant galleried **courtyard**, has a fine **facade** in smooth rustication divided by cornices and covered by large overhanging eaves. The ground floor entrance is flanked by a so-called "street bench" running along the pavement, on which in the 15th century wayfarers rested. The two upper floors are instead characterized by two rows of pedimented windows. The 16th-century facade overlooking the garden is attributed to Baccio d'Agnolo, who probably supervised the enlargement, wanted by the Antinori family, of the building's original structure.

CHURCH OF SANTI MICHELE E GAETANO

The church was built in the Longobard period, was called *San Michele Bertelde* in medieval times, and was radically transformed in the Baroque style from 1604. Numerous architects participated in this work of conversion, including Matteo Nigetti and Gherardo Silvani, who was also being responsible for the facade. The latter, built in pietra forte in 1648, rises in its measured monumentality at the top of a **flight of steps** according to the typical Baroque taste for perspective. Taking up Buontalenti's design for the facade of Santa Trinita, Silvani conceived a structure consisting of two orders one above the other divided by pilaster strips with Corinthian capitals.
The lower part is characterized by three pedimented portals surmounted by small niches and statues, while the upper part has a large round window framed by a monumental pediment and harmonious volutes terminating in line with the corner pilasters on which two enormous marble vases stand.
The **interior**, with a Latin cross plan and a single nave, repeats the decorative scheme of the Baroque facade based on the close relationship between architectural structure and figural ornament, which is enriched by the white marble statues executed by Giovan Battista Foggini and assistants.

At the end of Via Tornabuoni, the church of Santi Michele e Gaetano, a rare example of the Baroque in Florence, faces the classical forms of the facade of Palazzo Antinori.

PALAZZO STROZZI

In the second half of the 15th century the wealthy merchant Filippo Strozzi bought various properties in the area of what at the time was the Mercato Vecchio, today's Piazza della Repubblica, to build there his own residence, which he wanted to be larger and finer than both Palazzo Medici in Via Larga and the nearby Palazzo Rucellai. For this project he summoned Benedetto da Maiano, who, inspired by the buildings of Michelozzo planned a rectangular edifice, whose construction he was however unable to supervise. Filippo Strozzi subsequently sought other architects before finding in Cronaca the person who would complete the palace. The building designed by Cronaca had three particularly high storeys constructed around a central courtyard and a rusticated facade with two rows of elegant mullioned windows, and was crowned by a refined cornice of classical inspiration. In 1491 the ambitious merchant died, leaving his descendants the task of completing the palace. Strozzi's heirs respected their father's will and between 1495 and 1503 the three storeys planned by Cronaca were built. The work continued in stages until 1538, when they were interrupted following the confiscation of part of the palace by the Medici family, enemies of the Strozzi, to whom the property returned thirty years later. The complicated affairs of the family made the completion of the palace's southern side and the cornice impossible. Although unfinished, the building remained in the possession of the Strozzi family until 1937, when it passed to the National Insurance Institute which financed its restoration. Today it houses several prestigious cultural institutions like the **Gabinetto Vieusseux** and the **Institute of Renaissance Studies.**

PALAZZO DEI CAPITANI DI PARTE GUELFA

The palace was built in the 13th century, and during the bloody internecine feuds which were the scourge of medieval Florence housed the Captains of the Guelf Party, whose duties included the administration of goods confiscated from the Ghibellines and the maintenance of the city walls, public buildings and fortresses of the Florentine state.
In the course of the 14th century the building was enlarged in stages and given a covered **external staircase**, still visible in the modifications worked by Vasari around 1589. The lofty elegant Gothic two-arched window under the Guelf crenellation, which overlooks the small square below,

dates instead from the 14th century. In the first half of the 15th century Brunelleschi started to build a new structure over the 14th-century body, characterized by monumental arched windows surmounted by large oculi, but this was never finished. Unfortunately no trace of the Giottesque paintings which once decorated the interior remains, though we can still admire the fine **Sala dei Capitani**, dating from the beginning of the 15th century, and the **Salone del Brunelleschi**, whose coffered wooden ceiling is the work of Vasari, who also built the loggetta. The 14th-century portion of the Palazzo di Parte Guelfa, today the seat of prestigious city institutions, encloses the piazza of the same name, overlooking which is also the church, now deconsecrated, of **Santa Maria sopra Porta** (later San Biagio).

PALAZZO DAVANZATI

The palace was built in the 14th century as the residence of the Davizzi family who in 1516 sold the property to the Bartolini Salimbeni. It was later acquired by Bernardo Davanzati, a wealthy merchant and man of letters, who left it to his descendants in whose possession it remained until 1838. At the beginning of the present century the palace was bought by the antique-dealer Elia Volpi, who restored the exterior and recreated the original rooms inside, which he decorated with 14th-century furniture and objects, transforming the building into a museum of a medieval nobleman's house. The external **facade** was thus restored to its original splendour with its ground floor in rusticated stone and three portals with low arches, its three upper storeys graced by three rows of five-arched windows, and the open 16th-century loggia. Inside the building restorations were made to the fine **courtyard** and projecting **staircase** leading to the upper floors, where the large rooms reassumed their original appearance with frescoed walls, wooden ceilings and monumental wall fireplaces. Unfortunately the cost of this colossal work of recovery forced Volpi to sell a large amount of the furnishings and finally sell the palace, which in 1951 was acquired by the Italian state. In 1956 the palace became the **Museo della Casa Fiorentina Antica** , newly decorated with furniture and objects taken from the city's principal museums.

Museo della Casa Fiorentina Antica - Founded in 1956 inside Palazzo Davanzati, the museum houses furniture, paintings, sculptures and other objects arranged in such a way as to reconstruct the rooms of a Florentine nobleman's house of the 14th century. The entrance leads into the narrow courtyard, where a projecting staircase supported by large brackets and rampant arches goes up to the galleries leading to the upper floors. On the first floor is the large **Room of the Parrots**, probably used as a dining room, which gets its name from the distinctive decoration of the walls which are finished in imitation of refined medieval fabrics and characterized by numerous parrots. The **Room of the Peacocks**, on the same floor, was instead fitted out as a bedroom. The name of this room too comes from the refined wall decoration, in the upper part of which is a series of tre-

Museo della Casa Antica Fiorentina.

foil arches each containing the coat of arms of a family related to the Davizzi, the first owners of the house, and numerous birds, including peacocks. The room is furnished with a monumental bed dating from the second half of the 16th century, a carved wooden chest, in which clothes were originally kept, an 18th-century cradle and many other precious objects. On the second floor is the **wedding chamber**, whose walls are decorated with scenes inspired by the *Castellana di Vergy,* a French book famous in the Middle Ages, the **kitchen**, the **study**, and other rooms, all furnished with furniture, objects, paintings and precious tapestries.

CHURCH OF ST. MARIA MAGGIORE

Begun in the 10th century in Romanesque style, St. Maria Maggiore was almost completely rebuilt in Gothic style, at the end of the 13th century.
The linear severe **façade** has a lovely 14th-century *Madonna* of Pisan school on the pointed arch portal. The **interior**, in Cistercian style, is extremely simple: a nave and two aisles set in pointed arches on square pillars with cornices with dentils and square chapels. Traces of 14th-century frescoes by Agnolo Daddi, Spinello Aretino, Paolo Uccello and Masaccio can still be found on some of the walls. The two episodes from the *Story of King Herod*, painted in the style of Spinello Aretino in the **Sanctuary**, are particularly fine. In the left chapel is a relief in gilded wood of a *Madonna and Child,* while, in the right aisle, is a noteworthy altar on which is a painting of *Saint Rita* by the modern artist Primo Conti.

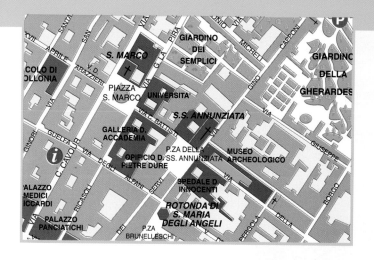

SS. Annunziata, S. Marco, and the Galleria dell'Accademia

The axis that unites Piazza San Marco, a lively meeting-place for students, with Brunelleschi's Santa Maria degli Angeli delineates the city's university area, which began to develop here in the 14th century. Historically, this area's singular propensity for culture and innovation saw important expressions in the religious field in the figure of the Reformist friar Savonarola, who held various posts at the Dominican monastery of San Marco. He was accused of heresy and burned at the stake in 1498 after having denounced the debasement of the secular and ecclesiastical institutions in his fiery sermons. Artistically, the expressions the area produced leave us much to choose from: the ritual pilgrimage to the Galleria dell'Accademia and Michelangelo's greatest works, a visit to Beato Angelico's frescoes in San Marco, and on and on, with visits

to the works by Brunelleschi, Alberti, Della Robbia, and Ghirladaio in Piazza Santissima Annunziata. The nearby Museo Archeologico is a fundamental point of reference for learning about Etruscan civilization.

PIAZZA SANTISSIMA ANNUNZIATA

The harmonious airy architecture of Piazza Santissima Annunziata is composed of three main buildings with colonnades that together form one of the most beautiful squares in Florence. Along the right side of the piazza as we look at the **church of Santissima Annunziata**, which gives the square its name, is the **Spedale degli Innocenti**, built in 1419 by Filippo Brunelleschi, while to the left is the **Loggiato della Confraternita dei Servi di Maria**, built by Antonio da Sangallo the Elder and Baccio d'Agnolo at the beginning of the 16th century in imitation of Brunelleschi's arcade opposite. Both buildings are reached by **flights of steps** leading up to elegant round arches resting on Corinthian columns in pietra serena.
Above the arches an architrave and string-course, also in pietra serena, mark the upper part of the structure, which is whitewashed and graced by rectangular windows surmounted by pediments. Another delightful feature is the row of splendid **Della Robbia roundels** in white and light-blue enamelled terracotta representing *Babies in Swaddling Clothes*, an allusion to the use of the old Spedale degli Innocenti as a foundling hospital, a function it performed for more than four centuries from the time of its construction. The square is also adorned with an *Equestrian monument to Grandduke Ferdinand I* by Giambologna and by two interesting 17th-century *Fountains*.

One of the two fountains by Tacca, the equestrian statue of Grand Duke Ferdinand I, and the Loggiato dei Serviti.

The portico in front of the facade of the church of Santissima Annunziata, and the Tabernacle of the Annunziata.

Gallery of the Spedale degli Innocenti - The five rooms of this small museum contain important works of the 15th and 16th centuries, including the splendid *Adoration of the Christ Child,* with the sweet serene figures of the worshippers, by Ghirlandaio (1488), the terra-cotta *Madonna and Child* (1488) by Luca della Robbia; the famous *Madonna and Child with St. John* (1460) by Botticelli; and an imposing *Madonna and Saints* by Pietro di Cosimo.

CHURCH OF SANTISSIMA ANNUNZIATA

Founded in 1248 as an oratory of the Servite Order on the site of an earlier votive chapel erected after the siege of Florence by Emperor Henry IV in 1081, the small building was originally dedicated to Santa Maria della Pace. The Servites instead traced their origins to seven rich Florentines (later venerated as the Seven Founding Saints) who, after the appearance of the Madonna on 15 August 1233, had retired in prayer to nearby Montesenario and founded a monastery called after the Servites of Mary. Just as the church's dedication was changed in 1314 to Santissima Annunziata because of a miraculous fresco by Fra Bartolomeo representing the Annunciation, so the original architectural structure was also radically altered. The church was in fact totally rebuilt between 1444 and 1481 by Michelozzo and other architects, including Antonio Manetti who on the advice of Leon Battista Alberti modified the original Michelozzian tribune which had in turn been inspired by the rotonda of Santa Maria degli Angioli designed by Brunelleschi.

The **tribune**, with its central plan and radial chapels, was thus used as a choir and its southern portion was joined to a longitudinal structure with a single nave and side chapels. The simple **facade** was later enriched with a **portico** of seven arches divided by six slender Corinthian columns with high pulvins, framed at the sides by elegant pilaster strips, following the model of Brunelleschi's arcade of the adjoining Spedale degli Innocenti. The middle arch was built by Antonio da Sangallo and decorated with the emblem of Leo X flanked by two frescoed figures by Pontormo, unfortunately now lost. The other arches of the portico were added at the end of the 16th century by Giovan Battista Caccini on the wishes of the noble Florentine Pucci family. Of the three doors under the portico the middle one admits to the so-called **Chiostrino dei Voti**, from which there is access into the interior of the church. The two side doors lead, on the right, into the **Pucci Chapel**, and on the left, into the **Chiostro dei Morti**, this too by Michelozzo, at the far end of which are the buildings of the old **convent of the Servites**.

Tabernacle of the Annunziata - In 1252, according to tradition, a certain Fra Bartolomeo was summoned to fresco the scene of the Annunciation on one of the walls of the church, a painting he promptly executed except for the Virgin's face, whose innocent beauty the artist felt unable to portray. Bartolomeo lay down dejectedly but on waking found the face miraculously portrayed in all its grace and purity. During the night, legend relates, an angel had painted in the delicate features of the Madonna. The prodigious event had such repercussions as to make the church the most venerated Marian sanctuary in the entire city and the painting one of the most invoked of all sacred images (as the numerous ex-votos prove). Towards the middle of the 15th century Piero il Gottoso had a marble tabernacle designed by Michelozzo built round it. This consists of four Corinthian columns and a rich trabeation supporting an elaborate Baroque canopy, added in the 17th century.

ROTONDA DI SANTA MARIA DEGLI ANGELI

This octagonal church was begun by Filippo Brunelleschi after 1433 but remained unfinished.
Designed after the architect's second journey to Rome, the church is inspired by the central-plan models typical of various classical buildings in the capital city. The structure has sixteen outer faces corresponding inside to eight chapels with two apses each.
In 1936 it was isolated from the buildings that in the meantime had totally engulfed it and was completely restored. At present it houses various departments of the adjacent Faculty of Letters and Philosophy.

MUSEO ARCHEOLOGICO

The Museum is housed in the rooms of the 17th-century Palazzo della Crocetta and contains archeological finds from various civilizations - those of the ancient Egyptians, Greeks, Romans and above all Etruscans. As an independent institution the Museo Archeologico dates from 1870, but the collections of antiquities belong to previous centuries. Cosimo il Vecchio and Lorenzo il Magnifico were in fact both enthusiastic collectors of classical marbles and bronzes, as well as ancient cameos, coins and medals. Their passion was shared by their grand-nephew Cosimo I de' Medici who considerably enriched the collections by adding to them many Etruscan bronzes, which from the 18th century were placed in a section of the Uffizi. Originally arranged in the Cenacle of Foligno, the collections, which had grown in the course of time thanks to successive acquisitions, were transferred to the present site in 1880. Among the Etruscan antiquities there are works of extraordinary beauty like the famous *Chimera*, together with objects of everyday use and furnishings which clearly testify to the refinement of this civilization, which showed particular interest in the after-life, as the interesting tombs and numerous sarcophagi demonstrate. Evidence of the Etruscans' intense commercial and cultural relations with the great contemporary civilizations of the Mediterranean is reflected in the celebrated *François Vase*, a product of Greek art discovered in a tomb near Chiusi.

ETRUSCAN ART
Chimera
(5th century BC)

The Chimera is one of the most celebrated Etruscan bronzes conserved at the Museo Archeologico. Found in Arezzo in 1555, it was immediately restored, possibly with the intervention of Benvenuto Cellini. It represents the mythical creature killed by Bellerophon which had a lion's body, a serpent's tail, and a ram's head on its back.

GREEK ART
François Vase
(6th century BC)

This vase, probably a wedding gift, came from the Athenian workshop of Ergotimos and was painted by the Greek artist Kleitias. It was discovered by Alessandro François in 1845 in an Etruscan tomb at Fonte Rotella near Chiusi. After being damaged as a result of a fall, it was restored in 1900 and is today one of the main attractions of the Museo Archeologico. Particularly interesting are the six rows of paintings inspired by episodes from Greek mythology.

CHURCH OF SANTA MARIA MADDALENA DE' PAZZI

The church and adjoining monastery, founded by Benedictine monks in the 13th century, were the object of extensive modifications in the following centuries culminating in the work of Giuliano da Sangallo that started in 1479 and lasted for over ten years. Departing from his own personal interpretation of Brunelleschian religious architecture, Sangallo created a building complex characterized by harmonious classical proportions that are clearly expressed in the fine **courtyard** in front of the church. This is surrounded by an arcade with Ionic columns (directly inspired by classical models) supporting a simple architrave. Of the old monastery, once occupied by the 'Convertite' or 'Penitenti' (from whom the church derived its original name, changed to the present one in 1699), several parts survive: the **chapter-house**, decorated with a celebrated fresco of the *Crucifixion* by Perugino, the **refectory** and the **cloister**, this also the work of Sangallo.

SYNAGOGUE

Following the destruction of the Ghetto and the old synagogues situated in the area of the city centre around the Mercato Vecchio, demolished in the 19th century to make way for Piazza della Repubblica, it was decided to build a new temple for the large Jewish community in Florence. Construction work started in 1874 under

the direction of numerous architects, including Mariano Falcini, Vincenzo Micheli and Marco Treves. The building, in which Moorish and Oriental elements are combined with the proportions of Byzantine architecture, was inaugurated in 1882 after the completion of the high cupola that blends admirably into the skyline of ancient Florence.

The courtyard in front of the church of Santa Maria Maddalena de' Pazzi, and the synagogue.

ARCISPEDALE DI SANTA MARIA NUOVA

This is the oldest hospital in Florence, originally founded by Folco Portinari, the father of the Beatrice celebrated by Dante, who had it built in 1286. The sick were taken care of by the sisters of the Oblate Order, whose convent stood next to the hospital.

Ten years later the **convent of Sant'Egidio** in front of the monastery of the Oblate was also acquired (of which the interesting small church survives). In 1312 a male hospital was annexed to it so that from then on the older institution was reserved for women only; the complex thus took the name of Santa Maria Nuova to distinguish it from the previous foundation, which was called Santa Maria. In 1606 the hospital was completely rebuilt, probably on a design by Buontalenti, by Giulio Parigi, who is attributed with the lower part of the facade with porticos, decorated at the level of the arches with splendid Medicean busts. The upper storey was added at the beginning of the 18th century. With the annexation of the old Camaldolensian monastery of Santa Maria degli Angeli in the 19th century the hospital reached its present size. The old convent of the Oblate remained operational until 1936, the year in which the city council bought it and turned it into a museum. This now houses, among other things, the **Museo di Firenze com'era** which is dedicated to the city's architectural and urban history and development.

CHURCH AND CONVENT OF SAN MARCO

Both the church and the convent were built by Silvestrine monks in 1299 on the site of an earlier oratory belonging to the Vallombrosan fathers. In the 15th century Cosimo il Vecchio persuaded Pope Eugenius IV to assign the entire complex to the reformed Dominicans of San Domenico of Fiesole and before their arrival he commissioned Michelozzo to enlarge the old convent and decorate the church. Cosimo and his grandson Lorenzo il Magnifico were always closely linked to the institution. They both made substantial donations that made possible further enlargements to the building and the foundation of a rich **library**. The long and interesting history of the convent was enriched in 1490 with a fundamental episode destined to leave its mark on the social and political life of the city: the return to Florence of Girolamo Savonarola, who in that year was elected prior of San Marco and began his vehement preaching against the Medici family and the corrupt ways of the city. The most conspicuous traces of Savonarola's presence at San Marco are now preserved in the **Prior's Quarter**, where he lived until 1498, the year of his death. The monastic complex has remained almost unaltered since then, a simple harmonious Renaissance structure built around two cloisters - the **Chiostro di Sant'Antonino** and the **Chiostro di San Domenico** - and comprising also, in addition to the monks' cells, the chapter-house, the Great Refectory, the Small Refectory and the Pilgrims' Hospice, now used to house the **Museo di San Marco** containing the precious works of another important friar of the monastery, Fra' Giovanni da Fiesole, better known as Beato Angelico.

Monastery of San Marco. From top to bottom, views of the Chiostro di Sant'Antonino, the Refettorio Grande, and the hall of the Ospizio dei Pellegrini with works by Beato Angelico.

Pilgrims' Hospice - This room was originally destined to accommodate pilgrims arriving in the city. It consists of a rectangular hall with cross vaults built by Michelozzo. Various paintings by Beato Angelico are kept here, including, on the end wall, the *Deposition* from the church of Santa Trinita.

Great Refectory - This was the original hall of the old Silvestrine convent which in the 15th-century was substantially modified by Michelozzo, who also added the powerful ceiling vaults. The end wall is dominated by the great fresco painted by Giovanni Antonio Sogliani representing the *Crucifixion*, above, and *Providence*, below.

BEATO ANGELICO
Crucifixion
(15th C.)
Chapter-house

Frescoed on the wall opposite the entrance to the chapter-house, this work reveals a conceptual innovation in the representation of the fact as a mystical vision: the Maries and St John are joined by numerous founding Saints of Orders contemplating the divine sacrifice. The lunette, in which we can admire the perspective composition immersed in an almost abstract landscape delineated by a bare mountain outline, is framed by a band punctuated by medallions with half-figures of the Saints and the Blessed of the Dominican Order and, in the frieze, by busts of Prophets.

Chiostro di Sant'Antonino - The work of Michelozzo is clearly discernible in the harmonious succession of graceful Ionic columns resting on a continuous low wall which, together with the open depressed arches, articulate the space of the portico in front of the windows of the cells once inhabited by monks. The lunettes formed between the insertion of the vaults and the corbels are frescoed with *28 Stories of Sant'Antonino* executed by 17th-century artists, including Poccetti, while some badly deteriorated *lunettes* by Beato Angelico have survived from the cloister's original decoration.

San Marco Prior's Quarter - Between 1490 and 1498 these rooms were inhabited by Girolamo Savonarola, the prior of San Marco during these years. The *Execution of Savonarola*, which took place in Piazza Signoria, is reproduced in one of the works kept in the vestibule of the Prior's Quarter, which also houses various portraits of the friar and other objects belonging to him - his cowl, sackcloths, books and some of his manuscripts.

The Last Judgment *by Beato Angelico
and the fresco of the* Crucifixion and
Providence *by Sogliani.*

Library of San Marco - This long room built in 1444 by Michelozzo is divided into three aisles by two rows of Ionic columns supporting round arches. The ceiling is formed by vaults of different
kinds: barrel vaults in the central aisle and cross vaults in the side
aisles. Completely restored in 1955, the library now contains
show-cases arranged along the aisles containing some of the *illuminated manuscripts* - numbering over a hundred pieces, including antiphonaries, psalters and graduals - which the museum houses in its extremely valuable collection.

GALLERIA DELL'ACCADEMIA

It was the Lorraine Grand-duke Pietro Leopoldo who founded the Accademia in 1784, endowing it with not only some fine statues but also a substantial collection of paintings that was amply supplemented with works removed from religious institutions which the suppression of the Orders and convents in the Napoleonic period had caused to come into the possession of the Grand-dukes. Subsequently rearranged and enriched by a section entirely dedicated to Modern Art, in the second half of the 19th century the Gallery was provided with a **Tribune** and **Salone**, a large room to house respectively the *David* and four *Captives* by Michelangelo, to which the *St Matthew* and, in 1940, the *Palestrina Pietà*, both by the same artist, were later added. In 1913 the Gallery of Modern Art was transferred to Palazzo Pitti, and the picture gallery was subsequently limited only to works belonging to Florentine painting between the 13th and 16th century. In the rooms of the picture gallery, the **'Sale Fiorentine'**, are important paintings by some great masters, including a *Madonna and Child* by Lorenzo Monaco, the celebrated frontal of a marriage-chest painted with a *Wedding Feast* by the Florentine school of the early Renaissance, and the *Madonna of the Sea* attributed to Botticelli. Of special note the new exhibit arrangement for the **Collection of Medicean and Lorenese musical instruments** owned by the Conservatorio Musicale L. Cherubini.

The Galleria dell'Accademia. The room containing the Rape of the Sabine Women *by Giambologna (copy).*

MICHELANGELO
Captives
(ca. 1519)

Originally intended to adorn the funerary monument to Pope Julius II in St Peter's in Rome, the Captives, four of which are housed in the Galleria dell'Accademia, were probably supposed to symbolize the liberal arts made prisoner by the death of the pope or even the provinces conquered by Pietro's resolute and warlike successor.

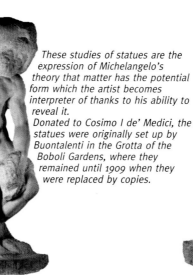

These studies of statues are the expression of Michelangelo's theory that matter has the potential form which the artist becomes interpreter of thanks to his ability to reveal it.
Donated to Cosimo I de' Medici, the statues were originally set up by Buontalenti in the Grotta of the Boboli Gardens, where they remained until 1909 when they were replaced by copies.

Michelangelo
Palestrina Pietà
(early 16th C.)

For centuries this marble statue was kept in a small grotto in a room adjoining the church of Santa Rosalia at Palestrina, near Rome. It was bought by the Italian state and moved to the Accademia in 1940. For many centuries believed to have been hewn directly from the rock, it was in fact sculpted from a large fragment of Roman cornice whose ornamental elements can still be seen in the rear part.

MICHELANGELO
(1475-1564)

Painter, Sculptor, Architect and Poet. Michelangelo was a highly versatile artist - sculptor, painter, architect and poet - who trained at the workshops of Florence, was esteemed by Lorenzo il Magnifico and was close to the leading Humanists of his time. He travelled a great deal, everywhere leaving extraordinary examples of his sublime art which was for long considered to be the perfect model of classical art itself: from the Vatican *Pietà* and the *Last Judgement* of the Sistine Chapel to the Captives and innumerable paintings. Perhaps his greatest achievement was that he succeeded in synthesizing a whole tradition stretching from the past up to Masaccio, re-elaborating the fundamental elements of it in a context of an emphatic and triumphant monumentality.

MICHELANGELO
David
(1501-1504)

On display in the Tribune, which forms an apse at the end of the central hall of the Accademia, is what may perhaps rightly be called Michelangelo's sculptural masterpiece and the symbol of the entire Renaissance and of Florence. Significantly a bronze copy of it was placed in the centre of Piazzale Michelangelo, the most panoramic location in the city. Obtained from a single block of marble, previously rough-hewn and abandoned in the courtyard of the Opera del Duomo because it was considered unusable, the statue was originally set up in Piazza della Signoria in front of Palazzo Vecchio, symbolizing, by alluding to the biblical episode of David's confrontation with the giant Goliath, the people's will to defend the small but powerful Florentine state and its liberty from every aggression, even by apparently greater powers. The statue was later removed from the square and replaced by a marble copy.

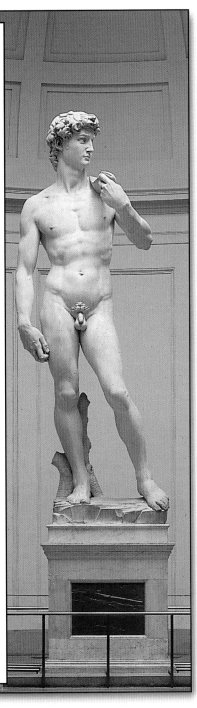

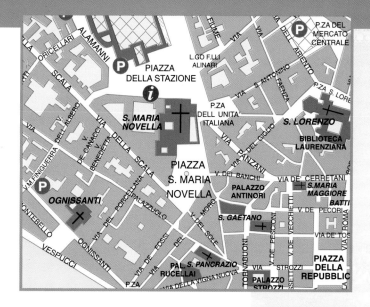

Santa Maria Novella

*T*he most important attraction on this itinerary is the basilica/cloister complex of Santa Maria Novella, which is in and of itself worthy of the name museum. The Dominican monastery of which it is part, in ancient times the religious complement to the Franciscan pole of Santa Croce, is an authentic masterpiece of the Gothic and Renaissance styles and is the heart of the district of the same name. The pietraforte travertine building of the railway station—designed by the "Gruppo Toscano" in the 1930's—is an organic part of the urban fabric of the historical city, the first example of Rationalist architecture in an area demanding a strong commitment to the urban environment like that dominated by the apse of the basilica of Santa Maria Novella. Near the station, the maze of medieval alleyways that separate it from Via Tornabuoni gives way, toward the outside of the old city, to the wide, straight streets of the 19th-century area that borders the Parco delle Cascine. In the direction of the Lungarno we find another integral part of this district, the ancient church of Ognissanti, with a Last Supper by Ghirlandaio in the refectory.

BASILICA AND CONVENT OF SANTA MARIA NOVELLA

In the first half of the 13th century medieval Florence received a decisive cultural, religious and urbanistic boost due to the development of the Mendicant Orders, which, a few years after their foundation, began to establish themselves within the city walls. One of the most important of these were the Dominicans, to whom in 1221 the Cathedral chapter donated the small oratory of Santa Maria delle Vigne, which had been built in 1094 over an earlier building of the 9th century. In 1246, under the direction of two Dominican friars, Sisto and Ristoro, work began on the enlargement of the original church and on the construction of a monastic complex that grew up around the **Chiostrino dei Morti.** In 1278 work began on the building of the church which, following the dictates of the Gothic style that had already been successfully applied in the remodernization of Santa Trinita, was completed in its vari-

ous parts, including the campanile and sacristy, around 1360 under the supervision of Fra Jacopo Talenti. In those same years the adjoining monastic complex witnessed a remarkable expansion, to the extent that it became one of the most important religious poles and cultural centres in Florence and, during certain periods, of the whole of western Europe. The **convent** grew up around two large cloisters: the **Chiostro Verde** - which led to the refectory and chapter-house, which was later converted into a chapel, the so-called **Cappellone degli Spagnoli** - and the **Chiostro Grande**, flanked by the library and the Cappella dei Papi. In the 15th and 16th centuries the various parts of the church and adjoining convent were rearranged and decorated with fine paintings and monumental fresco cycles by the greatest artists of the time.

The **facade**, initially left unfinished, was completed by Leon Battista Alberti in 1470. The tall spacious interior of the church adheres to a typical Cistercian design, a model which the religious buildings of medieval Florence conformed to in the 13th century. The Gothic style is recognizable in the tall clustered pilasters supporting pointed arches and cross vaults.

To convey a sense of greater depth Fra Jacopo Talenti progressively reduced the space between the pilasters from the facade towards the apse. The modifications made by Vasari between 1565 and 1571 did not radically alter the original Gothic design. Cosimo's architect limited himself to remaking some altars and reducing the size of the side aisle windows. With the passing of the years the wealthiest Florentine families, with their bequests and charitable donations, fi-

nanced the work of enlarging the convent and church, in the interior of which they had numerous chapels built where members of these illustrious families were buried. Of the chapels, all decorated with valuable works of art, we should mention the **Rucellai Chapel**, which once housed the famous *Madonna Rucellai* by Duccio di Buoninsegna, now at the Uffizi; the **Strozzi Chapel**, frescoed by Filippino Lippi; the **Cappella Maggiore**, decorated with frescoes by Domenico Ghirlandaio and the **Gondi Chapel**, containing a *Crucifix* by Brunelleschi, the only wooden sculpture made by the celebrated artist. In the **left aisle** is one of the greatest masterpieces of Santa Maria Novella and of Florentine Quattrocento art, the *Trinity* by Masaccio, a fresco painted by the artist in 1427. A recently-restored *Crucifix* by Giotto adorns the nave.

Facade - The facade was begun in the early years of the 14th century and initially only the lower section was completed. Work on it was finished in the following century by Leon Battista Alberti, who masterfully harmonized the pre-existing Romanesque-Gothic design with a new structure distinguished by the characteristic proportions and stylistic features of Renaissance architecture, of which he was an eminent theorist. The lower portion of the facade, with its blind arches and corner pilasters in black and white marble, reminds us of the Baptistery, while the four half-columns recall the facade of San Miniato. These features typical of Florentine Romanesque architecture are combined with elements of the Gothic style, such as the arches framing the recesses above the 'avelli' (family-vaults of Florentine nobles) and the side doors surmounted by ogival cusps. Alberti's work took its inspiration from this earlier portion, of which he maintained, for the upper part, the black and white marble decoration and the geometric proportions, and which he completed with the elegant classical portal. In the lunette is a painting of *St Dominic*, the founder of the Order to which the church and convent of Santa Maria Novella belonged. At the sides, above the aisle roofs, two scrolls continue the circular motif with two fabulously inlaid disks whose presence is both aesthetic and functional. The facade is further embellished with two astronomical instruments, an armillary

Details of the facade, in which original Gothic coexists harmoniously with the Renaissance elements of Leon Battista Alberti's plan, among which the circular lines of the rose window above the center portal and the curves of the two broad lateral volutes that link the upper and lower orders. The tympanum contains the circular image of the rayed sun, the emblem of the Dominican order.

sphere and a sundial, placed here in the 16th century by the Dominican father Egnazio Dati, the Medicean court astronomer.

Work on the facade lasted from 1458 to 1470 and was financed by Giovanni Rucellai, whose emblem, a billowing ship's sail, Alberti repeated in the frieze decorating the trabeation, above which the architect placed a high fascia with a decoration of square panels. The square, together with the circle, both expressions of harmony and symbols of geometric perfection, is in fact the recurring element of Alberti's facade. Above the fascia is a bay, corresponding to the nave, divided into three by black and white pilaster strips and with a round window in the centre. This is crowned by a triangular tympanum enclosing a flaming disk, the symbol of Christ.

Chiostro Verde - The cloister, which communicates with the piazza in front of the church by means of a Baroque portal, was built in the middle of the 14th century in forms that still reflect the Romanesque style, particularly evident in the sturdy octagonal pilasters in pietra forte and the broad depressed arches. It gets its name from the frescoes in terraverde illustrating *Stories from Genesis* which Paolo Uccello executed in the first half of the 15th century and which, detached in 1909 and in 1929, are today preserved in the adjoining refectory. The cloister leads through to the **Chiostro Grande**, this too characterized by octagonal pilasters and depressed arches supporting an open gallery with arches and elegant Renaissance columns. This cloister - flanked by the old library and the **Cappella dei Papi**, decorated with mural paintings by Pontormo - was completely frescoed with works by the greatest Tuscan artists of the 16th and 17th century. The northern side of the Chiostro Verde gives access to another important building in the complex of Santa Maria Novella, the Cappellone degli Spagnoli, the old chapter-house of the Dominican convent.

The Chiostro Verde of Santa Maria Novella.

MASACCIO
Trinità
(1427)

*The fresco was unknown to art historians until 1861, when the altar
that Vasari had built there in the course of modifications in the church
was demolished. It is certainly one of the most intense and significant
paintings in all Florentine art of the Quattrocento. Replaced in its original position after a long restoration, the* Trinità *can now be admired
in all its expressive vigour, which is built symmetrically according to a
pyramidal arrangement of the figures within a Renaissance architectural structure whose perspective effect was suggested to Masaccio by
Brunelleschi. At the top of the composition is God the Father, under
whom the crucified Christ acts as a fulcrum for the entire composition:
at the sides the figures of the Madonna and St John, at whose feet
are the donors, members of the Lenzi family. Below them the composition ends with a skeleton on a sarcophagus, a symbol of the transience of human life, to which the inscription above also refers: «Io fui
già quel che voi siete e quel ch'io son voi anche sarete».*

Cappellone degli Spagnoli. A detail of the cycle of frescoes by Andrea di Bonaiuto, Allegory of the Church Militant and Triumphant. One of the many interesting details is the view of the Duomo without its marble facing, as the 1367 plan by Andrea di Bonaiuto and other masters would have had it.

Cappellone degli Spagnoli - Originally used as the chapter-house, the vast room, covered by a superb cross vault resting on four octagonal corner pilasters, was built to the design of the Dominican Fra Jacopo Talenti around the middle of the 14th century. In 1540 the Spanish bride of Cosimo I de' Medici, Eleonora of Toledo, had it converted into a chapel so that her compatriots at the Medici court could attend religious functions.

In 1590, for this purpose, the small apse containing the altar was remade at the expense of the faithful Spanish community. Behind it a painting of *St James Healing a Paralyzed Man* by Alessandro Allori was placed, accompanied by a marble *Crucifix* and a fine polyptych by Bernardo Daddi representing a *Madonna and Child Enthoned with Four Saints*.

Around 1355 (and even earlier according to some scholars) Andrea di Bonaiuto, together with some assistants, executed a complex **pictorial cycle** in the chapter-house of the convent of Santa Maria Novella, for the most part inspired by the *Specchio della vera penitenza*, a work by Fra Jacopo Passavanti, the prior of that monastery. Passavanti probably also conceived the iconographical programme of the frescoes, whose aim was to glorify the Dominican Order in its guise as champion of the Faith and defender of Christian orthodoxy. Only in this way, by following Christ's example, was it possible to save one's soul and be reunited with God.

On the **wall facing** of the entrance the sacrifice of Christ is summed up in three scenes representing three fundamental moments in his life as a Man and as the Son of God: *Ascent to Calvary*, *Crucifixion* and *Descent into Limbo*. Illustrated on the four segments into which the vault is divided are Christ's triumph over Death (*Resurrection* and *Ascension*) and the first steps the Church makes in the persons of the Apostles, to whom Jesus conferred the mission of defending the Gospel on Earth (*Navicella* and *Descent of the Holy Ghost*).

On the **right wall** is the imposing *Allegory of the Church Militant*, with scenes of the mission and triumph of the Dominican Order. Opposite the 14th-century model of what the Duomo was supposed to have looked like, the civil and religious authorities - the Pope and the Emperor - rule the people and the Christian flock, which is in turn defended by dappled hounds, symbol of the Dominicans (*'Domini Canes'*, or the hounds of the lord) with their black and white robes. Further away, St Dominic, St Thomas Aquinas and St Peter Martyr refute the heretics, while at their feet hounds (Dominicans again) set upon wolves, symbolizing heretics. Higher up, the example of earthly joys, embodied by a group of dancing nobles, is set against that of penitence, the only real path towards Heaven, which St Dominic indicates. Those absolved are received by St Peter at the Gate of Paradise and two Angels crown the blessed, who are brought before Christ.

On the **left wall** is the *Triumph of St Thomas Aquinas*, who is celebrated here as a staunch defender of orthodoxy from heresies and as a doctor of the Church whose works conferred immense glory on the Dominican Order.

Cappellone degli Spagnoli. A cell of the vaulted ceiling.

Giovanni MICHELUCCI
(1891-1991)

Architect. Michelucci was an innovative and prolific architect, and a highly esteemed university teacher, who in his early career attempted to introduce the ferment of new European rationalism into the closed and conservative world of Italian architecture. Later, after the Second World War, he turned his attention to the insertion of modern architecture into historic settings. Among his most interesting creations are the **Central Railway Station of Santa Maria Novella** in Florence and the highly original **church of San Giovanni Battista,** better known as the *'Chiesa dell'Autostrada'*.

The front of the Santa Maria Novella railway station.

CENTRAL RAILWAY STATION OF SANTA MARIA NOVELLA

Florence's central railway station was built in 1935 by a team of architects under the direction of Giovanni Michelucci, who, basing his design on the principles of rationalist architecture, produced a structure combining functionality with noteworthy aesthetic qualities. The building makes considerable use of pietra forte, a stone typical of many Florentine buildings of the past, and complements perfectly the apse of Santa Maria Novella on the other side of the large square in front of it. The structure extends laterally and is distinguished on the outside by a projecting roof and on the inside by a glass-covered gallery, called the Galleria delle Carrozze, which leads to the railway platforms. Communicating doors connect the Galleria delle Carrozze with the large glass-covered departures hall, next to which is the refreshments hall decorated with two large *panels* by the painter Ottone Rosai representing two characteristic Tuscan landscapes.

CHURCH OF OGNISSANTI

The church was founded in 1256 by the Umiliati, a Benedictine Order, and was given the name of San Salvatore. It was completely rebuilt in the 17th century when the present facade was added, which Matteo Nigetti constructed in 1637 in a simple, linear Baroque style. It is divided by pilaster strips and characterized by two orders one above the other in which niches and windows are framed by fanciful architectural elements. Over the portal is a lunette representing the *Coronation of the Virgin,* a work in enamelled terracotta ascribed to Giovanni Della Robbia. The facade ends in an imaginative cornice bearing the city's coat of arms. In contrast to the rest of the building, the original campanile has survived, built between the 13th and 14th century on the model of that of Santa Maria Novella. The interior has a single nave, this also radically modified between the 17th and 18th century, and contains the *burial-place of Botticelli,* marked by a small round tombstone. The left arm of the transept leads through to the **cloister**, which is surrounded by the buildings of the old convent of the Umiliati which later passed to the Olivetans.

Cloister of Ognissanti - The cloister of Ognissanti, which can be reached both from the church and from the piazza in front of it, was built according to the stylistic canons of Michelozzo with Ionic columns and frescoed in the 17th century with *Scenes from the life of St Francis.* A portal joins the cloister to the old **refectory** of the convent, in which there are valuable frescoes by Botticelli and Ghirlandaio. Ghirlandaio painted the splendid *Last Supper* in 1480 for the choir of the church. On one side of the cloister is the entrance to the old chapter-house which is now a small museum containing liturgical objects.

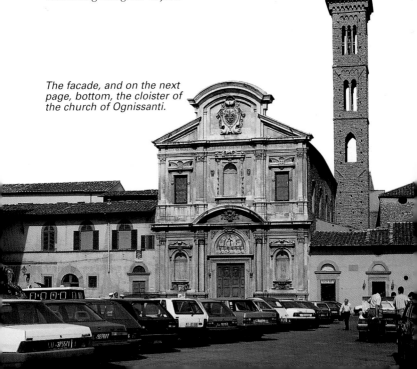

The facade, and on the next page, bottom, the cloister of the church of Ognissanti.

DOMENICO GHIRLANDAIO
Last Supper
(1480)
Refectory

This is one of the most intensely expressive frescoes which the artist painted, both for the serene atmosphere created by the pleasant landscape in the background, and for the figures of the Apostles, whose faces express a mixture of compassion for Christ's earthly destiny and solemn composure before the mystery of the Eucharist. The delightful landscape, with luxuriant fronds of trees peeping up from behind the wall and a cheerful fluttering of birds, has both a decorative and symbolic value; the peacock on the window, for example, symbolizes the regality of Christ, King of kings, Lord of Heaven and Earth. The fresco was painted by Ghirlandaio two years before the departure of Leonardo from Florence and seems to have inspired the master's Last Supper *in Santa Maria delle Grazie in Milan.*

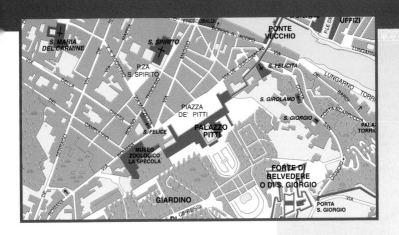

Oltrarno

*O*n the other side of Ponte Vecchio, the celebrated milieu of the shop windows of goldsmiths, silversmiths, and jewelers most loved by tourists, we venture into the tightly-woven fabric of narrow streets of the Santo Spirito and San Frediano neighborhoods, the home of the Florentine craftsmen's botteghe and many antique shops. The Oltrarno was known as a poor district destined to support "minor" activities since the times in which the inhabitants of the surrounding rural areas came to Florence through Porta Romana and settled here at the edges of the ancient city. And yet, the Oltrarno is home to such treasures as Masaccio's Cappella Brancacci in the church of Santa Maria del Carmine, and to Palazzo Pitti on the slopes of the lovely Boboli hill. The construction of this palace turned a page in the history of the district, which then began to fill with the homes of the lesser nobility. The grandiose Palazzo Pitti, the elected residence "di là d'Arno" of the Medici family for six generations, was (as it still is) linked to the political center "di qua d'Arno" by a private passage, the stupendous Vasari Corridor. In its Galleria Palatina, Palazzi Pitti preserves world famous art masterpieces and also provides the setting for important temporary exhibits.

CHURCH OF SANTA FELICITA

In the early centuries of Christianity this site was occupied by a cemetery and a church that was subsequently remodelled in the 11th and 14th centuries. Of this early building situated on the route of the *Roman Via Cassia*, which soon became the centre of urban expansion in medieval Florence, almost nothing remains today. In 1736 the church was completely rebuilt by the architect Ferdinando Ruggieri, who conserved only the lofty **portico** that Vasari had built to support the Vasari Corridor linking the Uffizi to Palazzo Pitti by crossing the Arno over Ponte Vecchio. The interior, with a single nave, contains some works of great artistic importance. In the **Capponi Chapel**, built by Brunelleschi but substantially modified in the 16th century, is the famous *Deposition* by Pontormo.

PALAZZO PITTI

When the architect Luca Fancelli, taking up a design by Brunelleschi in 1457, began the building of a residence along the slopes of the Boboli hillside for Luca Pitti he certainly could not have imagined that in later centuries the building would become the most majestic of all the Florentine palaces. The building originally consisted of a three-storey structure crowned by an open gallery whose width corresponded to the space occupied by the seven central windows of the present edifice. The building, which remained unfinished due to lack of funds, was bought in 1549 by Eleonora of Toledo, the wife of Cosimo I de' Medici, who wanted to make it the grand-ducal residence instead of Palazzo Vecchio, and who therefore provided for the enlargement of the original structure. This was done by Ammannati, who between 1558 and 1577 built a majestic

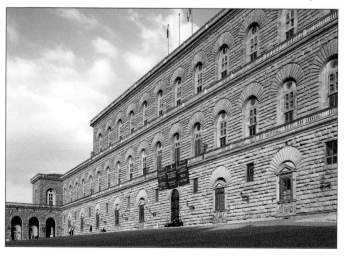

courtyard at the back of the building and closed all the entrance portals apart from the central one, inserting in their place fine pedimented windows resting on consoles.

In the first half of the 17th century the palace was further enlarged by Giulio and Alfonso Parigi, the former being responsible for the addition of three windows on each side and the latter for the extension of the ground floor to its present size. The two wings, commonly called the **Rondò**'s, with their porticoes and terraces, were instead added in the 18th century. The **Palazzzina della Meridiana**, facing the Boboli **Gardens**, dates to the Neoclasssical era and is home to an interesting **Costume Gallery**. After the Plebiscite for the annexation of Tuscany to the Kingdom of Italy, the palace was taken over by the House of Savoy and inhabited by this family throughout the period during which Florence was capital of Italy. In 1919 King Vittorio Emanuele III donated the palace and all the furniture and works of art contained in it to the Italian State, which provided for the arrangement of the collections in such a way as to form four separate museums: the **Galleria Palatina**, the **Gallery of Modern Art**, the **Museo degli Argenti** and the **Carriage Museum**, to which the **Royal Apartments** were later added.

Boboli Gardens - It was Eleonora of Toledo who commissioned this magnificent garden which stretches along the side of the Boboli hillside covering an area of about 45,000 sq. m. between Palazzo Pitti, Forte di Belvedere and Porta Romana. Its construction was begun in 1550 by Tribolo and continued by Ammannati and Buontalenti who worked on it from 1583. The latter was responsible for the so-called **Grotta del Buontalenti**, a picturesque and bizarre structure which he built between 1583 and 1588. In it are copies of the *Captives* by Michelangelo, the originals of which, now at the Galleria dell'Accademia, were arranged here in 1585. The walls are adorned with statues and frescoes that appear in the midst of calcareous concretions and shell decorations.

Facing, the facade of Palazzo Pitti; right, Buontalenti's Grotto and the amphitheater in the Boboli Gardens.

In line with the courtyard of Palazzo Pitti, opposite the **Fontana del Carciofo**, a 16th-century work by Francesco del Tadda, is the spectacular **Amphitheatre**, created by Alfonso Parigi in the 17th century to replace the original one consisting of modelled box hedges in which performances and festivities were always held. In the middle of this vast space, framed by flights of steps punctuated by a series of aedicules, is a large grey granite **basin** from the Baths of Caracalla in Rome and an Egyptian **obelisk** from the Temple of Ammon in Thebes. The entire garden is an endless succession of flower-beds and lawns lined with trees and hedges and decorated with statues and fountains, some of them works by famous artists of the 16th and 17th centuries, forming a spectacular and picturesque whole that makes this one of the loveliest gardens in the world.

The **Palazzina del Cavaliere** hosts the **Museo delle Porcellane**, with its magnificent collection of porcelains of Sèvres, Chantilly, Vienna, Meissen, Worcester, and other centers of production.

GALLERIA PALATINA

The fame of Palazzo Pitti is linked mainly to the Galleria Palatina, in which works of great value are collected, including numerous masterpieces by the most famous Italian and foreign artists. The paintings are displayed in sumptuous rooms according to those museographical criteria, substantially aimed at creating a picture gallery for personal and family use, which inspired the collectionism of both the Medici and Lorraine families. The works are in fact arranged in a purely decorative way, in such a way as to form compositions of strong visual impact in settings that harmonize well with the lavish stuccoes and paintings that decorate the ceilings of the various rooms. It was Cosimo II de' Medici and his son Ferdinando II who created the splendid picture gallery in the first half of the 17th century, commissioning to Pietro da Cortona and Ciro Ferri the decoration of the rooms according to iconographical subjects of mythological and allegorical inspiration. The collections were later enriched by various Grand-dukes who purchased or inherited numerous works. In 1828 Leopoldo II of Lorraine opened the Gallery to the public, a total of fifteen rooms which increased with the passing of time until the picture gallery reached its present size. The Gallery houses numerous works which are a fine representation of the entire artistic panorama between the 15th and 18th centuries. Particularly important is the nucleus formed by the paintings of Titian, such as *The Concert*, and Raphael, by whom there are splendid portraits such as *The Veiled Woman*, *Maddalena Doni* and *'La Gravida'* alongside religious subjects like the *Madonna of the Grand-duke*, the *Madonna of the Chair*, the *Madonna 'dell'Impannata'* and the *Vision of Ezekiel*. The Florentine school is represented by Filippo Lippi (*Madonna and Child*) and by Andrea del Sarto (*Assumption with Apostles and Saints*, *Holy Family* and *Stories of Joseph*). There are also important works of 17th-century Italian art like the *Sleeping Cupid* by Caravaggio, and of North European art represented by paintings by Rubens, including *The Four Philosophers* and *The Consequences of War*.

Filippo LIPPI
Madonna and Child
(ca. 1452)

This tondo, probably painted for Lorenzo Bartolini, is a work of exceptional quality, remarkable for the play of perspective and for the distinctive background which the artist succeeds in using as a setting for two episodes from the life of Mary: the meeting of Joachim and Anne, and the birth of the Virgin.

RAPHAEL
Madonna of the Chair
(1515)

This tondo shows a scene of deep intimacy that focuses on the figure of the Child. The influence of classical art is perceptible in the plasticity of the forms, but the intensity of the colours clearly betrays the influence of Venetian painting. The work belongs to Raphael's Roman period and is one of the most popular by the artist.

149

RAPHAEL
Madonna of the Grand-duke
(1504-05)

In 1799 this painting was bought from an antique-dealer for Grand-duke Ferdinando III of Lorraine, who was so fond of it that he wanted it with him always and hung it above his bed when it was not with him on his travels. His descendants were also attached to the picture, to the extent that, when in 1859 Leopoldo II was forced to abandon Florence on exile following the Plebiscite for the annexation of Tuscany to the Kingdom of Italy, he refused to be separated from it and took it with him to Vienna where it remained for many years.

RAPHAEL
The Veiled Woman
(1516)

Vasari, who saw this work in the house of the merchant Matteo Botti, claimed that it was a portrait of the only woman loved by Raphael. In this work the artist confidently demonstrates an acquired maturity and the constant presence of influences from Venetian painting. Like the Madonna of the Chair, *this work is also traceable to Raphael's Roman period and represents one of the highest expressions of the Italian Renaissance*

TITIAN
The Concert
(1510-13)

For a long time believed to be a work by Giorgione, but since last century attributed to Titian's early period, this painting represents a young Augustinian monk turning his face towards a clergyman holding a lute. On the other side of him a young man with a plumed hat seems to be listening. The poses of the three figures appear highly studied and confer to the scene an atmosphere of solemn theatricality.

CARAVAGGIO
Sleeping Cupid
(1606)

Painted in Malta, this work represents the god Eros as a child peacefully sleeping on his fatal arms of passion: the bow and arrows with which he sparks off love. The typical mix of pigments is characterized by a refined play of chiaroscuro that seems almost to materialize out of nothing the delightful figure of the god, whose features however draw deeply on reality.

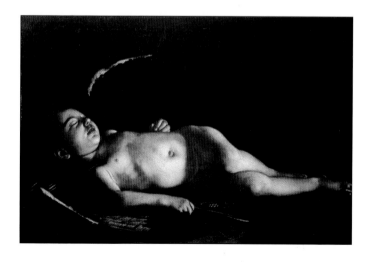

Pieter Paul RUBENS
The Four Philosophers
(1606)

The four figures represented here are from the left: Rubens, his brother Philip, Justus Lipsius and his pupil Jan van Wouwer. The scene probably refers to a lesson on Seneca, whose bust is shown above. Here Rubens shows all his skill as a portraitist through a psychological introspection of the characters, obtained by means of intense facial expressions that seem almost to involve the onlooker in the dialogue.

Modern Art Gallery - Situated on the second floor of Palazzo Pitti, it consists of over 2000 works of sculpture and painting by artists active between the beginning of the 19th century up to the early decades of the 20th century. The Gallery covers many rooms: the first of these contain works in neoclassic and Romantic style, with imposing historical paintings; among these art works, mention must be made of the *Bust of Napoleon* by Canova in **Room IV**, the large group of *Cain and Abel* by Duprè in **Room X**, various fine portraits by Antonio Ciseri in **Room XII**, and works by the great Giovanni Boldini in **Room XV**; *The Rain of Ashes* by Gioacchino Toma, *Beach near Barletta* by Giuseppe de Nittis and others are in **Room XVII**. **Rooms XXIII** and **XXIV** contain a rich collection of works by the most important Macchiaioli painters: Silvestro Lega, Giuseppe Abbati, Telemaco Signorini, Cristiano Banti, Edoardo Borrani, Vincenzo Cabianca, Cesare Ciani, to name only the best known. Room XXIII also contains some of the outstanding works by the father of the Macchiaioli movement, Giovanni Fattori.

Museum of Silverware - The first three rooms are decorated with
allegorical and trompe-l'oeil frescoes by Michelangelo Colonna
and Agostino Micheli. The fourth room is frescoed with allegories
exalting the *Deeds of Lorenzo the Magnificent*. The Museum contains examples of household and religious objects in precious met-
als, bowls and splendid vases in semi-precious stone and rock crys-
tal, as well as marvelous ivories and the vases from the collection
of Lorenzo the Magnificent. The **Treasure** is exhibited in another
room. It includes rare jewels and the jewelley collection of Anna
Maria Luisa Ludovica, the last of the Medici.

MUSEO BARDINI

Collections of paintings, period furniture, precious tapestries, Roman
archaeological finds, weapons, and wooden sculptures. Especially interesting are a *Bust of Saint John* by Andrea Sansovino, a marble
Charity by Tino di Camaino, and a number of della Robbia terracottas. The museum is currently closed for restoration.

LA SPECOLA

The old **Palazzo Torrigiani** in Via Romana took the name of *Speco-
la* from the astronomical and meteorological observatory that Pietro
Leopoldo of Lorraine, Grand-duke of Tuscany, set up here in the second half of the 18th century. In 1775 Pietro Leopoldo also founded
here a **Zoological Museum** which houses rich zoological and botani-
cal collections, including examples of stuffed animals,
some of which are now practically extinct,
and one of the most famous collections of anatomical wax models in
the world, created between the 18th
and 20th centuries. In 1841, for the
congress of Italian scientists,
Leopoldo II of Lorraine had built on
the first floor of the building the **Tri-
buna di Galileo**, a room richly decorated with marbles, mosaics and frescoes celebrating the progress achieved
by Florentine scientists, primarily Galileo,
whose statue stands at the end of the hemicycle.

A view of Porta Romana from outside the walls.

PORTA ROMANA

The ancient *Via Cassia* linking Rome with Siena and then Florence entered the city through this very gate, which therefore was called "porta romana". It is built into a powerful tower erected in 1326 and still has its enormous wood and wrought-iron doors. Inside, above the arch, a fresco of the 14th century representing a *Madonna and Child with Four Saints* is still visible. The gate formed part of the only stretch of that sixth line of walls (the third of the system of fortifications of medieval Florence) which were built between 1284 and 1333 and almost totally demolished in the 19th century

CHURCH AND CONVENT OF SANTO SPIRITO

In the 12th century, in the area of Oltrarno known as *Caselline*, a small scantily-populated hamlet consisting of a few houses standing in the middle of green fields, stood a small church where the Augustinian Order chose to establish its monastery in 1250. This was the foundation date of the convent of the so-called Hermits of St Augustine, monks from the small monastery of San Matteo di Arcetri situated in the hills to the south of Florence, who in 1269 began the construction of a new church and the enlargement of the original monastery, which by this time was expanding at the same time as the development of the Oltrarno district, of which Santo Spirito became the nerve centre. In 1428 Filippo Brunelleschi received the commission to rebuild the old church, which had been destroyed by fire. Work, however, began only in 1444, after the idea of building the new church with its facade facing the Arno river had been dropped. Brunelleschi readopted the essential style of San Lorenzo but built a structure of greater austerity that was more consistent with his theoretical principles. The building of Santo Spirito, left unfinished by its architect, who died in 1446, provided for the construction of numerous spaces within a single structural unit in which the principle of circularity was dominant. All this was achieved by doing away with all rectilineal masonry in favour of circular shapes and open surfaces, alternately concave and convex: curved chapels running right round the perimeter of the building, and the separation of the nave and aisles with 31 identical columns supporting round arches and lateral half-columns. This fundamental principle was also adhered to in the church's ground-plan, which grafts the basilical model onto one with a central plan, the latter having a **cupola** designed by Brunelleschi in 1444, but actually executed thirty years after his death. Unfortunately the builders who continued working according to Brunelleschi's original design departed partially from the master's theoretical principles in completing the church, which was concluded in 1487 except for the **facade** which remained unfinished.

To the left of the church is the **Cenacolo** of Santo Spirito which houses the collection of sculpture of the Fondazione Romano.

Campanile of Santo Spirito - In 1566 the campanile of Santo Spirito was finished according to the designs of Baccio d'Agnolo, who had worked on it from 1503 to 1517, raising the structure from the pre-existing base which was built in 1490. The construction has two storeys, characterized by large pedimented windows, and ends in an elegant belfry, which is narrower compared to the body below it and characterized by corner buttresses with volutes. The pyramidal cusp was added in 1541.

The clean lines of the facade of the church of Santo Spirito.

CHURCH OF SANTA MARIA DEL CARMINE

In 1268 a donation was made by the Florence municipal authorities to the Carmelite Order of a site in Oltrarno, not far from the monastery of Santo Spirito. Around the convent of the Carmelites developed the secular life of the area, which also expanded urbanistically between the two monasteries. The church was originally built in the Romanesque-Gothic style, still identifiable along the flanks of the present building, adjoining a fairly run-down area which the Signoria converted into a square in 1317 on the request of the Carmelites themselves.

As part of the programme of architectural and urban renewal promoted by Cosimo I de' Medici, also the church of the Carmine, which had been finished in 1476, was subjected to restorations that were completed by Vasari in 1568. The **Corsini Chapel**, dating from the Baroque period, was executed by Pier Francesco Silvani in the second half of the 17th century in honour of Sant'Andrea Corsini, the 14th-century bishop of Fiesole. In 1771 the church was destroyed by a violent fire that spared only the facade, the sacristy, the superb **Brancacci Chapel** and the chapel of Sant'Andrea Corsini. This was the pretext for a modernization of the church, the interior of which was rebuilt in the Baroque style and completed in 1782. The sober 18th-century architecture of the interior, characterized by pilaster strips and side chapels is enlivened by the trompe-l'oeil decorations executed by Stagi and Romei on the vaults of the nave and transept.

BRANCACCI CHAPEL

The chapel, situated at the end of the right arm of the transept, was built before 1386 and frescoes for it were commissioned by Felice Brancacci in 1425. The financial standing of the patron, a wealthy businessman, ambassador in Egypt, and an important figure on the Florentine political scene in the 15th century, enabled him to entrust the decoration of the chapel to Masolino, and shortly afterwards also to Masaccio, who finally replaced Masolino

Cappella Brancacci, a detail of Masaccio's Tribute Money; *opposite page, above, a detail of Masolino's* Saint Peter Healing the Cripple.

in the execution of the frescoes which were interrupted in 1427. The summoning of Masolino initially, and of Masaccio from Rome subsequently, and the death of the latter in 1428, probably prevented the work from being completed. The exile of Felice Brancacci, banished from Florence in 1436 for his overtly anti-Medicean policy, marked their definitive suspension. Fifty years later, between 1481 and 1485, the decoration of the chapel was resumed and completed by Filippino Lippi, who, following Masaccio's style, completed the pictorial cycle dedicated to *Stories from the Life of Saint Peter*. The iconographical scheme, combining scenes from the life of St Peter with *Original Sin*, focuses on the figure and mission of the first pope of the Christian Church, starting with the *Preaching of the Apostle*, the *Baptism of the Neophytes*, and the

MASACCIO
Tribute Money
(1426)

The fresco refers to the episode of the Gospel in which Christ and the Apostles are stopped by a tax-collector who asks them for tribute money. Christ, respectful of earthly laws, shows Peter a lake where he will find a fish with the money in its mouth to be given to the tax-collector. The Tribute Money is the first monumental scene of Renaissance painting, the supreme expression of the results of Massaccio's research into perspective and his meticulous study of the psychological dimension of portraiture. The volumetric and syntactical characteristics of the group are in fact intrinsically linked to define the content of the story and the evocative quality of the scene. The human figures simultaneously determine their own inner space by means of an intense expressive charge and give meaning to the surrounding space whose perspective scheme they themselves coordinate. The serene face of Christ, to which the almost adolescent and classically measured figure of St John shows the closest resemblance, is the narrative centre and compositional fulcrum of the scene. Around Christ the anxious expressions of the assembled Apostles convey their expectancy of the miracle, on which they confer all the importance and solemnity due to it as a key event in the great Christian epos.

numerous *Miracles* worked by him in the course of his apostolate, continuing with his *Imprisonment in the Mamertine* in Rome, the *Visit of St Paul* and the *Liberation from Prison by the Angel*, and finishing with the saint's *Martyrdom*. These frescoes, together with the Trinity of Santa Maria Novella, are Masaccio's greatest masterpieces, the *Tribute Money* particularly being the expression of the artist's full maturity. The rival attraction, the masterpiece of Masolino, is the *Healing of the Lame Man* and the *Resurrection of Tabitha*.

The interior of the church of Santa Maria del Carmine.

MASOLINO
The Healing of the Lame Man and the Raising of Tabitha
(1425)

Painted on the wall opposite the Tribute Money, this fresco, with its spatial assonances and harmonious perspective lines, seems somehow to anticipate the great fresco by Masaccio, who appears to have worked as an assistant on this work by the master.

The background had been attributed to Masaccio, though today it is thought to be by Masolino, with the houses and streets of 15th-century Florence, a successful example of the artistic transcription of everyday reality and city life achieved by means of a masterful play of volumes and colour which marks the real beginning of Renaissance painting. Here too the fulcrum of the composition is the human figure, whose centrality is admirably expressed in the two passers-by - the rich, elegant clothing, the postures and the expression of the faces, whose composure and poise convey the moderation and vigour of the cultural environment in which Masolino and Masaccio lived and worked.

CHURCH OF SAN FREDIANO IN CESTELLO

This church occupies an important place in the context of 17th-century Florentine architecture, which, although changing the essential lines of Roman Baroque, found its own characteristic style consisting of simpler and more austere forms to which the autocthonous Renaissance and Mannerist tradition was not estraneous. It was in fact the Florentine Gherardo Silvani who originally designed the church, his work being continued by a Roman architect, Cerutti, who took over its supervision in 1690. The building was then completed by Antonio Maria Ferri, who also designed the cupola, whose high cylindrical drum is divided by pilaster strips. The Latin cross *interior* is solemnly laid out according to the dictates of Baroque architecture and has fine side chapels decorated by the most important Florentine painters of the 18th century. The facade, which has an unfinished appearance, faces the Arno river (just as Brunelleschi had originally designed the church of Santo Spirito). The church gives onto a piazza along the riverbank enclosed by two other interesting buildings: the **Great Seminary**, also known as 'del Cestello', and the **Granary of Cosimo III**, a large but elegant building attributed to Foggini.

THE HILLS OF FLORENCE — FIESOLE

*T*he hills to the north and south of Florence embrace the city and gently force it to stay close to its river. They set the natural limits to urban expansion, but merit is also due to a city planning policy that has aimed at safeguarding the integrity of the green scenario that is as much a part of Florence as the city itself. One characteristic of these hills is their closeness to the city center, above all in the Oltrarno area, where, immediately behind Palazzo Pitti, the Boboli Gardens spread up the slope. Likewise, it is only a few minutes' walk up Costa San Giorgio and the "Rampe" to such splendid observation points as San Miniato, Forte Belvedere, and the final destination of any sights-minded visitor to Florence, Piazzale Michelangelo. The Bellosguardo hill, also south of the city, offers a little-known panorama of Florence that is nevertheless among the most suggestive. To the north, the Fiesole hill is constelled with ancient villas immersed in greenery and, although the bell tower of the Duomo is easily distinguishable to the eye, the tower it is actually much further from the center of Florence than it seems. Whether made on foot or by trolley, the "passeggiata a Fiesole" was a ritual for the Florentines of times past. Fiesole has always been a reality unto itself, and proud of being older than Florence. The Museo Archeologico preserves many Etruscan finds and the Roman theater, which every year provides the stage for the internationally-famous Estate Fiesolana festival, with cinema, theater, and concerts, is one of Italy's most panoramic.

PORTA SAN GIORGIO

This gate belonged to the fifth line of city walls (the second of medieval Florence) built between 1125 and 1175, walls which in this stretch also formed part of the subsequent fortifications built between 1284 and 1333. In its present form, reduced in height compared to its original dimensions, the gate dates from around 1260. The 13th-century capitals have survived and on the outside above the supporting arch is a stone bas-relief of 1284 representing *St George.*

A bas-relief with the figure of Saint George.

FORTE DI BELVEDERE

In 1544, at the time of the war against Siena, Cosimo I de' Medici had the defensive walls of Florence reinforced by fortifying the ramparts raised about a decade before by Michelangelo. In the following years he continued to strengthen the defensive line, but it was only around 1569 that on the summit of the hill of San Giorgio the construction of a fortress was begun. However, it was not until 1590 that Grand-duke Ferdinando I de' Medici commissioned the architect Bernardo Buontalenti to rebuild completely, on the basis of more modern and effective defence criteria, what would become the *Fortress of Santa Maria di San Giorgio in Belvedere*, more commonly known as Forte di Belvedere. The star-shaped construction consists of four main bastions with recessed flanks and spurs and two auxiliary bastions and is graced by the elegant **grand-ducal Palazzina.**

The whole structure is designed as an arrangement of planes on various levels that ensured from every point a complete view of the city below and the surrounding hills. This principle also inspired the architecture of the palazzina, being clearly noticeable in

the distinctive arrangement of the windows and the invention of the double loggia facing two opposite directions, an interesting foretaste of Palladian structural devices. From the palazzina, the terrace below and the bastions one can admire a splendid panorama with picturesque views of the most important Florentine monuments.

PIAZZALE MICHELANGELO

The reorganization of the city promoted at the time when Florence was the capital of Italy involved an expansion of the urban fabric beyond the physical limits hitherto defined by the walls, and a revolutionizing of the very concepts of the city that had characterized the evolution of medieval and Renaissance Florence.

The old bastions and city walls, only short stretches of which survive today, were demolished and replaced by a ring-road suitable for the passage of vehicles. This consisted of broad avenues, modelled on those of other great European cities, punctuated by large squares built around those city entrance gates that had remained standing after the demolition of the perimeter walls. Undoubtedly the most impressive of the numerous interventions carried out was the creation of a long avenue, known as **Viale dei Colli**, along the slope of the hills behind the southern part of the city, and the building of a vast square dedicated to the great Renaissance artist in one of the most panoramic spots in the entire environs of Florence. Both were built between 1865 and 1870 on a design by the architect Giuseppe Poggi, who also designed the flights of steps connecting the square with the riverside avenues below. In 1875 the **Monument to Michelangelo** was erected in the centre of the square, from where one can admire a spectacular view over the entire city. The Monument consists of bronze reproductions of some of the artist's major works preserved in Florence: the David of the Galleria dell'Accademia and the statues decorating the famous Tomb monuments of the Medici Chapels.

CHURCH OF SAN MINIATO AL MONTE

It was on this very hill, originally called *Monte Fiorentino*, that the early Christians found refuge and set up their first cemetery, in which, at the time of the persecutions of the Emperor Decius, Minias was buried, the saint and martyr whose relics soon became an object of worship. On the site of that old Christian cemetery con-

The mosaic of the facade of the church of San Miniato al Monte.

taining the saint's remains a small church was built whose existence is documented from the time of the Carolingian period. The cult of St Minias received renewed impetus around the year 1000 following the diffusion of a hagiography that claimed he was an Armenian king who for obscure reasons had found his way to Florence and had been martyred in the city following a long series of tortures from which he had miraculously emerged unscathed. After being beheaded in Florence, Minias, carrying his own head, walked up Monte Fiorentino where he finally lay down to rest and entered the ranks of God's elect. The saint's new fame caused Bishop Hildebrand in 1018 to promote the construction of a new

San Miniato al Monte. One of the most beautiful facades in Florence, atop the Monte alle Croci hill.

church on the site of the old paleo-Christian building. Thus, by the hands of unknown artists, builders and stone-dressers, one of the most impressive expressions of Florentine Romanesque architecture and one of the most beautiful monuments in the entire city was created. Work on the construction of the basilica, which was flanked by a convent of Benedictine nuns, went on for almost two centuries. The adjoining **Bishops' Palace**, begun in 1295, was used as a summer residence of the Florentine bishops until in 1594, after having served as a headquarters for the Spanish troops under the command of Cosimo I de' Medici, it was incorporated into the convent of San Miniato which had been taken over by the Olivetans in the 14th century. The reconstruction of the campanile, which had collapsed, was begun in the 16th century. The **interior** of San Miniato still has its original basilical structure consisting of a **crypt**, or underground church, in which the saint's relics are preserved, and a

San Miniato al Monte. The upper portion
of the facade; below, the free-standing
Cappella del Crocifisso.

presbytery or tribune, situated in the area of the apse and raised above the crypt and nave, which is reached by means of two flights of steps at the end of the two side aisles. The nave and aisles are separated by columns with fine capitals, some of them from Roman buildings, supporting round arches. The triumphal arch, dividing the nave from the presbytery, is decorated like the facade with original geometric motifs in green and white marble. The trussed roof is painted, while the pavement is characterized by 13th-century panels with marble inlay representing signs of the zodiac and symbolic animals. At the end of the nave is an elegant tabernacle known as the **Cappella del Crocifisso**. The stairs at the end of the right aisle also lead to the **sacristy**

Facade - The facade was built in the course of the 12th century and covered with alternating green and white marble to form a harmonious geometric design typical of Florentine Romanesque architecture and found in other buildings of the period, as can be seen, for example, in the Baptistery. The facade of San Miniato is divided into two orders. The five arches of the lower order, supported by Corinthian half-columns, contain real entrance portals alternating with false portals in green and white marble. The upper order is decorated with four pilaster strips in the part corresponding to the nave, and adorned with geometric elements in the parts corresponding to the side aisles. A pedimented window in the classical style was built into the central portion at the end of the 12th century. In the following century, above it, a **Mosaic** with a gold background was inserted representing the *Enthroned Christ in the act of blessing the Virgin and St Minias*, who is shown offering his king's crown to the Saviour.

The large apse mosaic of the church of San Miniato al Monte.

A large pediment decorated with small arches and other geometric motifs crowns the facade, at the top of which towers an *Eagle* holding a small bale of rolled cloth, the symbol of the Wool Guild which from 1288 administered the basilica.

Cappella del Crocifisso - At the end of the nave, in line with the crypt, we find this splendid **tabernacle** that was commissioned by Piero il Gottoso from Michelozzo in 1448 to house the famous *Crucifix of St John Gualberto*. The tabernacle has the shape of a classical aedicule with barrel vaults resting on Corinthian columns and pilasters, with a decorated coffered ceiling and roof made by Luca della Robbia in white and blue enamelled terracotta highlighted in gold. The Crucifix is kept behind the fine door panels decorated by Agnolo Gaddi at the end of the 14th century with the figures of *Saints Minias and John Gualberto* and with *Scenes of the Passion*. The figure of St John Gualberto Visdomini was one of the best-loved and venerated in Florence. A young Florentine knight, who had decided to avenge the murder of his brother, met the assassin in front of the abbey of San Miniato. But moved by pity he forgave him, and entering the church prostrated himself at the foot of a crucified Christ, whom he saw making a gesture of assent. The knight promptly donned the monk's habit and became a staunch supporter of the purest evangelical precepts, which he put into practice together with a group of fellow brothers with whom he retired to Vallombrosa in the Tuscan Apennines and founded the Vallombrosan Order.

Presbytery - The presbytery, or tribune, consists of that raised part of the church, closed by screens and built near the absidal area, which was used to house the monks. Being more spiritually elevated than the congregation, for whom the nave and aisles below were reserved, the monks took their places in the stalls around the altar, from where they followed the liturgical functions singing psalms and sacred hymns. The presbytery is divided by four columns into three aisles and surrounded by a marble screen enclosure built in 1207 and characterized by panels and rosettes elegantly decorated with inlaid polychrome marble. Behind the fine Romanesque altar dating from the 11th-12th century, an enamelled terracotta *Crucifix* attributed to Luca Della Robbia stands out against the elaborate semi-circular apse divided by blind arches resting on green marble columns and by niches containing large rectangular windows covered by thin slabs of pink marble. A mosaic with a gold background dating from 1297 embellishes the absidal vault. In it we find the image of the *Enthroned and Blessing Christ* surrounded by the symbolic figures of the four *Evangelists* (the *winged Lion* of St Mark, the *Eagle* of St John, the *winged Ox* of St Matthew and the *Angel* of St Luke) and by portraits of the *Virgin* and *St Minias.* The inclusion of two trees, a fig and a palm respectively, and of various animals placed at the two ends of the mosaic lends a naturalistic touch to the solemn theatrical scene.

Crypt - The large crypt, which dates from the 11th century, is divided by a veritable jungle of thirty-six slender marble columns and by four powerful columns added later to support the presbytery above. A place of contemplation and prayer for the monks of the adjoining convent, the crypt, the vaults of which are decorated with various frescoes by Taddeo Gaddi, contains the *relics of St Minias,* which are arranged in the fine altar decorated in bichrome marble in 1018.

Sacristy - The sacristy of the church of San Miniato is a large square room with a cross-vaulted ceiling built in 1387. Immediately after the date of the building the spaces formed by the vaults and by the lunettes below were frescoed by Spinello Aretino and assistants. While the vaults were decorated with the figures of the four *Evangelists*, the large lunettes were decorated with images of the *Stories of St Benedict,* illustrated in two rows of panels each containing an episode from the saint's life.

San Miniato al Monte. Elegant details in marble.

*On these pages,
images of the interior
of the sacristy,
frescoed by Spinello
Aretino.*

SPINELLO ARETINO
Stories of St Benedict
(after 1387)
Sacristy

The frescoes, executed by Spinello Aretino and assistants, are arranged in two rows with scenes characterized by a bare incisive narrative style that makes this work the artist's undisputed masterpiece. Of the various episodes drawn from the life of St Benedict particularly noteworthy in terms of composition and the splendid use of colours is the one of the Saint leaving his family accompanied by the wet-nurse and the following miracle with St Benedict giving back to the wet-nurse the whole tray that she had dropped and broken. In line with the two previous scenes, in the lower row we find the episode in which St Benedict reproaches Totila, who had put him to the test by exchanging himself with his groom but who was immediately recognized, and the intensely moving Death of the Saint.

On the fine wooden stalls, dating from 1472, are some interesting works including a 15th-century *Reliquary-bust of St Minias* in gilded wood and a full-figure *Statuette of St Benedict* of clear Della Robbia workmanship.

A detail of Scenes from the Life of Saint Benedict *in the sacristy of San Miniato al Monte.*

CERTOSA DEL GALLUZZO

The **Certosa del Galluzzo** or of *Florence in val d'Ema* was founded by Niccolò Acciaioli when he decided to construct a monastery in Florence that was "*lo più notabile loco a tutta l'Italia*" (the most remarkable place in all of Italy). The monastic complex, which dates from the end of the 14th century, lies on the summit of a hill, where the Ema and the Greve rivers run together. There are two churches and a series of rooms connected to them (cloisters, friars' cells, refectory, chapter room), in addition to the large crenellated building known as **Palazzo degli Studi**, which was intended as a hall of residence for Florentine youths and where they would be prepared in the liberal arts. The **main Church** is a large building with a single nave and cross vaults, slightly pointed, which spring from composite piers "*multipli et uni*" set against the walls, forming a sort of framework which articulates the space in a restrained rhythm. This structure is still visible despite the modifications carried out over the centuries, above all inside, which was literally covered with stuccoes, marble and frescoed intonaco, and in the façade, remodelled at the end of the 16th century in forms that already tended towards the Baroque. The second **Church** of the Charterhouse, Greek-cross in plan, is an extremely elegant example of a typically Florentine Gothic style, which has undergone only slight modifications. For the most part, the other rooms of the Charterhouse date from the Renaissance, in particular the **Cloisters**: the one in the centre, with arches on Corinthian columns, and the two smaller cloisters with Ionic capitals in the style of Brunelleschi.

An aereal view of Certosa del Galluzzo.

FIESOLE

A view of archeological area.

Today's territory of Fiesole is very different from what the city used to control in ancient times. Numerous finds of the Etruscan civilisation have come to light in the vast area, north of the Arno, between the Sieve and the Ombrone rivers: among these finds are the so-called "Fiesole stelae", which date from the 6th century BC. In addition to these, finds from prehistory, of the early Iron Age and of the Copper and Bronze ages, have been unearthed. It is thought that the Etruscan settlement of Fiesole was at the centre of a populated area overlooking the Florentine valley. The prosperity of Etruscan and Roman Fiesole was probably due to the fortunate geographical position: near a point of the Arno that could easily be forded (Florentia also would have been built near here) and close to the Apennine passes that connected this area with the Valley of the Po. It is supposed that the territory of the Roman Municipium of Fiesole extended mostly to the north of the Arno, while the "colonia" of Florence to the south. It was occupied by the Ostrogoths and the Byzantines, and from the 6th century was the site of a Lombard settlement, as documented by the remains of a necropolis. In 1125, after three military campaigns, Florence conquered Fiesole, destroying part of the ancient walls.

THE RUINS OF ANCIENT FIESOLE

Traces of this period include various parts of the strong **city walls** and the ruins of a one cella **Etruscan Temple** with wings and two columns in the pronaos. Since part of it is till standing, it can be considered as one of the finest examples of this kind in Etruria.
A considerable number of interesting finds from the Etruscan period - *urns, bucchero*, clay and bronze *statuettes* - together with Roman objects can be seen in the **Museum** near the archaeological site.
Fiesole was invaded by the Gauls in 225 BC and captured by Marcus Porcius Cato in 90 BC; in 80 BC it was occupied by Silla and turned into a military colony. This was when Fiesole became a Roman city (*Faesulae*) with a forum, temples, theatre and baths.
In the **Theatre**, which is still well preserved, you can sometimes assist to classical plays and it can hold about 3000 people. It dates from the beginning of the Imperial age and it was embellished during the periods of Claudius and Septimius Severus.
The **Baths** also belong to that period and were restructured by Hadrian. The remaking of the Etruscan **Temple** is of Republican times (1st century BC).

CATHEDRAL

Fiesole, set between the two hills of San Francesco and Sant'Apollinare, is, today, one of the most admired places in the environs of Florence. Among the city's historical edifices, the most remarkable is the Cathedral, dedicated to *Saint Romulus*. It was begun during the 11th century, and finished and enlarged later. During the 19th century, it was restructured and restored, especially the façade and the tower. The **interior** is on a basilican plan, with a nave and two aisles divided by round pillars - some have salvaged Roman capitals - and a large semi-circular apse. The presbytery is raised for the existence of a big **Crypt** beneath it - this same structure can be observed in the Basilica of San Miniato al Monte, near Florence.

Piazza Mino da Fiesole - To the left of the Cathedral is the **Rectory**, originally 11th-century, but rebuilt during the first half of the 15th century. The **Palazzo Vescovile** was also begun in the same period, but completed in the late 17th century, from which also dates the nearby **Seminary**. The large square, named after *Mino da Fiesole*, is closed by **Palazzo Pretorio**, set on a slight high ground, and, to the east, by the **Church of Santa Maria Primerana**. The first is a picturesque edifice, prevalently 15th-century in style, and with a slender porch with architraves. The church has a 16th-century porch in front.

Sant'Alessandro - The ancient Basilica of Sant'Alessandro lies almost at the top of the steep road leading to the summit of the hill of San Francesco. Originally, it was the site of an Etruscan temple, then replaced by a Roman one, and finally, by the Christian church. Its origins are said to go back to Theodoric and it may have inherited the capitals and columns of the Roman temple. The pre-Romanesque origins are almost certain, although the church was restored during the 11th century and remodelled during the 16th and 18th centuries.

The Convent of St. Francesco - It stands on the summit of the hill. This was once the site of an Etruscan necropolis, followed by a Roman one, and later the site of the medieval fortress destroyed by the Florentines in 1125. Founded at the beginning of the 14th century, as the headquarters of the Florentine hermits, it passed to the Franciscans in the early 15th century. They enlarged the **Church** - which today has a long narrow nave with barrel vaults - and the **Convent**, of which Saint Bernadino of Siena was abbot.

BADIA FIESOLANA

This abbey stands on the site of the old Cathedral of Fiesole dedicated to Saint Peter, on the steep road that from Ponte alla Badia, on the *Faentina Road*, climbs to St. Domenico. The Camaldolites replaced the original church with another, of which we can still admire the **façade**, decorated in green and white marble in a style similar to the one of San Miniato al Monte. From the middle of the 15th century, thanks to the generosity and will of Cosimo the Elder, the church and most of the complex were restructured. Cosimo himself lived in the **Convent**, which has an elegant *Cloister*. He had his personal quarters built, and collected rare illuminated codexes, which passed to the Laurentian Library, in 1778, when the convent was suppressed.

LUNCHTIME

EATING OUT IN ITALY AND TUSCANY

This introduction is dedicated to our visitors from other countries, since Italians take for granted much of the information that follows.

Italians enjoy their lunch break differently from most other Europeans and indeed the rest of the world: they don't cotton to the one-dish meal, since they are used to choosing among a vast assortment of dishes including antipastos or appetizers, first courses, meat and fish entrées, a vegetable, fruit, and dessert. In Italy, sitting down to table is above all a taste experience, and the diner assembles his meal from the myriad of items listed in the various menu categories—and, of course, adds a libation chosen from a good wine list. The dishes are not "with" anything; that is, when you choose a dish, and in particular a main course, you are not automatically served a vegetable, which you will select from a separate menu category. A full meal made up of all the courses is generally a great deal of food. Most foreign diners will find they can eat well by choosing, each according to his taste and experience, just an entrée and a vegetable, or an appetizer—or a first course—followed by a meat or fish entrée. Fruit and dessert are, obviously, extra pleasures that can be skipped at the end of an already full meal. Italian menus are organized by courses, and the price of each dish is listed alongside it One characteristic Tuscan cooking has in common with all Italian and Mediterranean cuisine in general is that it valorizes the intrinsic flavors of the ingredients, which are rigorously natural. Sauces, finishing touches, and garnishes are of secondary importance in any Tuscan dish. In Florentine and Tuscan cooking, the "gourmet quality" of a dish lies in its very simplicity, and the derives from the special attention paid to preserving the original flavors of the elements that go to make up the dish, which must always be enjoyed "as is" and never smothered in extraneous sauces; even extra seasoning should be used with discretion. This "severity" (which if we look closely is only apparent) guarantees that the diner will enjoy to the full a cuisine that is healthy and delicious and portions that are almost always generous.

WHERE TO EAT

Florence offers many different types of eating places: trattoria, ristorante, enoteca, spaghetteria, or pizzeria. The trattoria is a typically Italian institution of lower-class origin (but now much in vogue) where service is minimal but the quality of the food is excellent. The ristoranti, where you'll often find international as well as local cuisine, offer first-class dishes and fine—at times truly top-notch—service. The enoteche, of which there aren't all that many, are high-class establishments where you can taste excellent wines of the very best vintages and often accompany them with food prepared using typical products. Lately, especially among the younger set, the spaghetterie are very popular: as the name implies, their menus offer mainly pasta dishes. And don't forget the eternal pizzerie, where you can choose among infinite types of pizza and, quite often, excellent pasta dishes.

Oil and Wine

Florentine (and, in general, Tuscan) cooking is simple and natural,. The usual condiments are therefore almost exclusively olive oil and the fat released by the food itself; added fats of animal origin (butter, cream, etc.) are the (infrequent) exception. Tuscany is one of the most important world producers of olive oil. Tuscan oil is protected and controlled from the planting of the olive trees through pressing of the oil: the result is a light, tasty, easy to digest, and dietetic oil. The term "extravergine" means that the acidity of the oil (strictly from the first pressing) is less than 1% (the top grade: extra-virgin). Tuscan wines are superb. The best known worldwide is the red controlled-origin Chianti wine produced in the region of the same name between Florence and Siena and in contiguous areas. The outstanding Brunello di Montalcino is the centerpiece in a diadem of other great red wines ideal for accompanying roasts and grilled meats (including the bistecca): Bolgheri-Sassicaia, Carmignano, Morellino di Scansano, Pomino, and Vino Nobile di Montepulciano. The blue-ribbon controlled-origin white wine, perfect with fish dishes, is the Vernaccia di San Gimignano, but there are also Ansonica Costa dell'Argentario, Bianco dell'Empolese, Bianco della Valdinievole, Bianco di Pitigliano, Bianco Pisano di San Torpè, and Candia dei Colli Apuani from which to choose. Other fine white and red wines are labeled Capalbio, Colli di Luni, Cortona, Montecarlo, Montecucco, Monteregio di Massa Marittima, Orcia, Parrina, Sovana, Val d'Arbia, Val di Cornia, and Valdichiana. "Vino novello," or new wine, is a very young red tapped and bottled only a month after pressing and sold beginning in early November. Perhaps the best known of the dessert wines is the dry or sweet **vinsanto**, a raisin wine made from partially-dried grapes and aged lengthily in special sealed "caratelli" (small casks), ideal for dunking cantucci and other dry biscuits. Other fine dessert wines are the smooth Moscadello di Montalcino and the Aleatico wines produced on Elba and on the Argentario peninsula. Attention! The prices of vintage bottles of these wines may surprise you. Ask before ordering.

DINING IN FLORENCE

dining suggestions and dishes you will find in
Florence's trattorie and other eating places

LEGENDA

Bold = Florentine dish
Bold italic = Tuscan dish
Italic = Italian dish
* = seasonal dish

FLAVOR:
A sweet-sour **D** mild **M** average **S** tasty/hearty **P** spicy

ANTIPASTI (Appetizers)

1-Crostini M-S Slices of French-style bread spread with different toppings. The typical Tuscan crostini are topped with a pâté made of chicken livers, onion, capers, and anchovies. Often served with affettati and other crostini topped with porcini mushrooms and by fried polenta topped with ragù ("**crostini misti**"). If the "support" is a toasted slice of bread from a full-size loaf, we have a *crostone*: this is not an antipasto, but rather a sort of entrée (try the crostoni with beans or lardo di Colonnata).

2-Fette col cavolo nero* **S** Boiled black cabbage served on toasted slices of Tuscan bread rubbed with garlic, moistened with the cabbage water and drizzled with olive oil. Tuscan black cabbage, with its very dark green, curly leaves, is also an essential ingredient in ribollita, and is available from October through March.

3-Fettunta* (or Bruschetta) **S** Slices of Tuscan bread, toasted and rubbed with garlic and drizzled with extra-virgin olive oil. The best time to enjoy this simple delicacy is in autumn, with freshly-pressed olive oil. In summer, the bread may be rubbed with sun-ripened tomatoes.

4-Caprese* **M** Rounds of mozzarella (preferably from buffalo milk) alternating with slices of tomato, garnished with basil and dressed with olive oil (May – September).

5-Insalata di mare (or Antipasto di mare) **M** Poached crustaceans and mollusks cut into bite-size pieces and served with a dressing of oil, lemon, parsley, and salt and pepper. Some restaurants also serve hot or cold fish appetizers of their own creation.

6-Prosciutto e melone* **S** Wedges of cantaloupe (called "**popone**" in Tuscany) served with sliced prosciutto toscano (June – September).

AFFETTATI

Affettati (or Antipasto della casa) **S** Platter of pork cold cuts and sausages: usually composed of finocchiona or sbriciolona, salame, and prosciutto, but may also include capocollo, spalla, and soprassata (see explanations below). The **Antipasto misto** toscano also includes crostini and carciofini and other vegetables, pickled or preserved in oil.

• **1 Capocollo** A flavorful, briefly-cured sausage made with cuts of neck and shoulder meat. According to place, sometimes called **coppa** or a variant thereof.

• **2 Finocchiona** A briefly-cured sausage of ground fatty and lean cuts of pork flavored with garlic and wild fennel seeds. The so-called **sbriciolona** is a large finocchiona made with more coarsely-ground meats.

• **3 Prosciutto** Ham, salt-cured for a medium-long period. Tuscan prosciutto differs from that of Parma and of San Daniele as to color, texture, and, above all, its more distinctive flavor.

• **4 Salame** Salami: generally, an air-dried sausage cured for a medium period, made of finely-ground lean meats seasoned with wine, garlic, and sugar, mixed with cubes of fat and peppercorns. Tuscan salami is compact but not hard, with a very intense fragrance.

• **5 Soprassata*** (or Soppressata) Head cheese: a sausage of coarsely-cut bits of meat (usually pork) from the boiled and boned head, seasoned with spices, garlic, and citrus rinds and packed in cloth into a firm jellied mass. Eaten fresh, from October through March.

• **6 Spalla** A "prosciutto" made with the front leg of the pig. Smaller and less prized, but just as tasty as true ham.

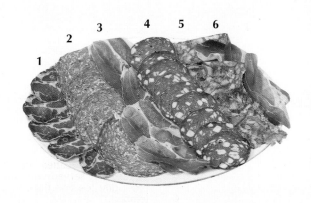

PASTA

Bucatini

Linguine or trenette

Chiocciole or conchiglie

Eliche

Tagliatelle or fettuccine

Tortellini bolognesi

Cannelloni

Long dry pasta
Bucatini
Fusilli lunghi
Linguine or trenette
Perciatelli
Spaghetti alla chitarra
Spaghetti or vermicelli, spaghettini
Ziti

Short dry pasta
Chiocciole or conchiglie (shells)
Eliche
Farfalle (bow-ties)
Fusilli (spirals)
Mezzani
Orecchiette
Assorted soup pasta
Penne, smooth and ridged, pennette
Rigatoni
Sedani
Tortiglioni

Egg Pasta
Lasagne
Tagliatelle or fettuccine (noodles)
Tagliolini (thin noodles)

Filled Egg Pasta
Agnolotti (Piemonte) (filling: meats, processed pork products, onion, egg, and nutmeg)
Cannelloni (filling: ricotta and spinach)
Cappelletti (Romagna) (filling: capon, ricotta, parmigiano, egg, and nutmeg) and Cappellacci
Maltagliati, strisce, toppe, or stracci (pasta cut by hand while fresh into irregularly-shaped pieces)
Pansotti (Liguria) (filling: greens and herbs)
Passatelli (Romagna)
Ravioli (Emilia) (filling: ricotta and spinach)
Tortelli di patate
Tortellini (Bologna) (filling: meats, processed pork products, and parmigiano) and Tortelloni

Spaghettini

Spaghetti or vermicelli

Fusilli

Penne lisce and rigate

Tortiglioni

Farfalle

Cappelletti romagnoli

SAUCES AND PASTA TOPPINGS

"Ajo and oio" **P** Garlic sautéed in olive oil until just golden, parsley, and hot red pepper. The cooked spaghetti is the tossed in this mixture in the pan.

Amatriciana **S** Sauce for bucatini, made with bacon, onion, tomato, parsley, and olive oil.

Boscaiola **M** Pasta sauce made with chopped porcini mushrooms sautéed briefly with garlic and parsley; cream is sometimes added.

Carbonara **S** Spaghetti topping made with egg, sautéed bacon, and pepper. The hot pasta is tossed in the mixture to cook the egg and served immediately.

Carrettiera **P** Spaghetti topping made with pomodoro, much hot red pepper, and parsley.

Pesto **S** Ligurian sauce made of basil pounded with cheese, pine nuts, and olive oil; generally served over linguine or "trenette."

Pizzaiola **S** Sauce for penne made with pommarola, mozzarella, capers, anchovies, and oregano.

Pommarola **M-S** Tomato sauce with garlic, carrot, onion, celery, herbs, sugar, salt, and olive oil.

Puttanesca **S** Topping for spaghetti or fusilli made with bacon, tomato, capers, black olives, olive oil, and pecorino cheese.

Ragù (or *Sugo di carne*) **S** Meat sauce: a pasta topping made of beef browned in olive oil and sautéed carrot, onion, and celery, simmered together at length with tomatoes.

Salsa di noci **S** Topping for pansotti, made of walnut meats, soft bread crumbs, garlic, and olive oil (cream is sometimes added).

Salsa verde **S** Sauce made of parsley minced with capers, hard-boiled egg, vinegar, and olive oil; generally served with boiled meats.

"Sulla nana," "sul cinghiale," "sul coniglio," "sulla lepre," etc.
S Dialectical Tuscan names for pasta toppings made, respectively, with duck, wild boar, rabbit, hare, etc.

PRIMI PIATTI (First Courses)

1-Carabaccia M Soup of onions cooked in broth, served over toasted bread with parmigiano.

2-Crespelle alla fiorentina (or Panzerotti) **M** Crêpes filled with a mixture of ricotta cheese and spinach seasoned with nutmeg; covered with Béchamel sauce and tomato sauce and baked until crusty on top.

3-*Gnocchi* **M** Balls of potato, egg, and flour (**Topini**), boiled, and served "alla bava" with fontina cheese, or with a sauce of gorgonzola cheese. The so-called "gnocchi verdi" (green gnocchi, a name erroneously ascribed to the gnudi) also contain spinach or herbs. "Gnocchi alla romana" are rounds cut from "sausages" of semolina prepared with milk and eggs, and cooked au gratin with a topping of parmigiano, bread crumbs, and nutmeg.

4-*Lasagne al forno* **S** Strips of egg pasta arranged in layers with Béchamel sauce and ragù and baked until crusty brown on top.

5-Minestrone **M** Soup of chopped vegetables (greens, carrots, cabbage, onions, beans, celery, potatoes, zucchini, etc.) with or without pasta or rice, served hot or cold.

6-*Paglia and fieno* **D-M** White and green taglierini ("straw and hay" egg noodles) tossed with cream or served al pomodoro.

7-Panzanella* S Cold summer first course made with mois-tened bread crumbs, onion, tomato, and basil tossed with oil, vinegar, and salt and pep-per (June – September).

8-Pappa al pomodoro* S Thick
soup made of bread simmered
with local tomatoes, garlic,
basil, and olive oil (June – August).

9-Pappardelle sulla lepre M Egg
noodles, wider than tagliatelle,
served with hare sauce. Pappardelle are also served with
ragù, game sauces, or boscaiola
style. In mountainous areas like
the Lunigiana region, chestnut
flour is often added to the pappardelle dough.

10-Penne strascicate S Penne
drained "al dente" and reheated
with ragù. Penne are also served
boscaiola style, pizzaiola style,
with crabmeat, and in many
other sauces.

11-*Ravioli* **M** Squares of egg pasta
filled with a mixture of ricotta
cheese and spinach, seasoned
with nutmeg (but the filling may
also be made with wild greens,
mushrooms, fish, truffles,
squash, etc.). Usually served
with ragù or with butter and
sage (but the topping will vary
according to the filling). The so-
called "raviolo aperto" (open
ravioli) is a large square of pasta
served with various "fillings"
and toppings.

179

12

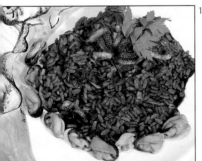

13

14

15

16

12-Ribollita S Bread soup with "cavolo nero" (Fette col cavolo nero), beans, and assorted vegetables. It is usually prepared the day before, boiled again, and served slightly cooled.

13-*Risotto* **M-S** Rice cooked with sautéed onion, broth, and other ingredients (asparagus, chicken livers, mushrooms, etc.) and brought to a creamy consistency through the addition of butter and parmigiano. Saffron lends the yellow color to "risotto alla milanese." **Risotto ai carciofi*** (with artichokes) is typically Tuscan. "Risotto di mare" is made with garlic and parsley (instead of onion), mollusks, and crustaceans. The so-called "riso nero" (black rice) is colored with squid ink.

14-*Spaghetti allo scoglio* **S** Spaghetti tossed over high heat with mollusks and crustaceans, garlic, parsley, hot red pepper, and olive oil. Besides with butter, "ajo and oio," carrettiera, *carbonara, pomodoro, or puttanesca toppings, spaghetti (or vermicelli), which exalt the flavors of seafood, are also served "alle vongole" (with clams) or "alle vongole veraci" (larger clams), or with other types of clams (notably the smaller arselle and telline), all'astice (European lobster), al granchio (crabmeat), or alla bottarga (salted, pressed fish eggs).

15-Tortelli di patate S Similar to large ravioli, filled with a potato-and-egg mixture, served with ragù or other sauces. Meat-filled tortelli are a specialty of the Maremma region; in Versilia, we find "tordelli" with mixed meats and vegetable filling.

16-*Zuppa di farro* **S** Thick soup made with farro (a type of primitive wheat resembling barley, typical of the mountains of the Garfagnana region), beans, garlic, mixed vegetables, herbs, and olive oil.

SECONDI PIATTI DI CARNE (Meat Entrées)

1-Arista al forno S Pork loin (with bone), roasted with garlic, rosemary, sage, and fennel seeds

2-Bistecca alla fiorentina S T-bone beef steak (with fillet and bone), at least two fingers thick (1 1/2 in), weighing about 1 kg (2 1/4 lb)(the price is given per hectogram: 1/10 kg), grilled, usually "al sangue" (extra rare). Due to the outbreak of "mad cow disease" (bovine spongiform encephalopathy), the classical Fiorentina is now boned. The steaks of the Chianina breed of beef cattle are among the world's tenderest and tastiest.

3-Bistecchina di maiale S Loin or rib pork chop (lombatina or costoletta), grilled or pan-fried with garlic, rosemary, fennel seeds, and olive oil. This entrée is sometimes called "braciola di maiale," but the term "braciola" more properly applies to a slice of meat, especially from the shoulder cut known as "scamerita." Pork chops are often served with cavolo nero (in season) (black cabbage). The meat of the Cinta Senese breed of pigs is excellent.

4-Carpaccio S Strips of raw meat sprinkled with rucola and slivers of grana cheese and drizzled with oil and lemon juice. Bresaola (dried salt beef), cheeses, salmon, swordfish, etc. may also be prepared "in carpaccio."

181

5

5-Fegato alla fiorentina S
Floured slices of veal liver fried in olive oil with garlic and sage. Liver "alla veneziana" is cooked with onions simmered in white wine and olive oil.

6-*Filetto all'alpina* **M** Beef or veal tenderloin grilled with a porcino mushroom cap and seasoned with garlic and parsley. Other recipes for tenderloin: with green peppercorns, with juniper berries, "in crosta" (en croûte), with balsamic vinegar, etc.

6

7-Ossobuco alla fiorentina S Osso buco (slices of shin of veal, with marrow bone) stewed with tomatoes and often served with piselli alla fiorentina or spinach. In Lombardia, osso buco is prepared "in gremolada" (that is, with a sauce seasoned with garlic, parsley, anchovy, and lemon rind) and served with risotto alla milanese on the side.

7

8-Pollo alla cacciatora S Chicken casseroled with garlic, rosemary, sage, tomatoes, olive, red wine, and olive oil. Another fragrant chicken dish is "pollo al finocchio" or "affinocchiato," with garlic, sage, bacon, and a healthy dose of fennel seeds. Chicken is also served roasted, "alla diavola" (grilled with garlic, herbs and seasonings, oil, and lemon juice), or prepared "al mattone" in a special terracotta container.

8

8

9-Polpettone S Meat loaf: a breaded "salami" of ground beef, soft bread crumbs, chopped dressed pork products, egg, parmigiano, and parsley, browned in olive oil and often cooked with tomato sauce.

10-Rosticciana S Fatty pork spareribs, grilled.

11-Salsicce e fagioli S Pork sausages cooked on top of the stove with tomato, garlic, sage, and boiled beans.

12-*Tagliata* M Grilled beef entrecôte, served cut in pieces with aromatic sauces, salad (assorted small-leaved and wild greens), or slivered raw porcini mushrooms.

13-Trippa alla fiorentina S Pre-cooked white tripe (rumen and honeycomb stomach of beef), sautéed in oil with vegetables, stewed with tomatoes, and served sprinkled with grated parmigiano. "**Trippa e zampa**" calls for adding a boiled, boned veal foot. In summer, boiled tripe is served cold tossed with minced mixed vegetables, garlic, parsley, oil, and vinegar ("**insalata di trippa**").

SECONDI PIATTI DI PESCE
(Fish and Shellfish Entrées)

1-*Baccalà alla livornese* S Batter-fried desalted salt cod reheated in tomato sauce with garlic and parsley. Salt cod is also served blanched with boiled chick peas, batter-fried, cooked with leeks in tomato sauce, and "in zimino"; that is, with greens (* seppie in zimino). According to locality, stockfish or dried cod may be used in place of salt cod.

2-*Cacciucco alla livornese* P A soup or stew (a one-dish meal) of various fishes (scorpionfish,

gurnard, hound fish, weever, etc.), crustaceans, and mollusks, cooked with garlic, tomato, parsley, and hot red pepper and served over toasted bread rubbed with garlic. One variant on the traditional recipe is the excellent "cacciucco alla Viareggina" of the Versilia coast.

3-*Frittura di mare* (or Frittura di paranza) S Assorted small fish and small calamari, young fish and fry (like whitebait), squid rounds, etc., dredged in flour and deep-fried.

4-*Impepata di cozze* **P** Mussels opened in the pan over high heat with garlic, oil, parsley, and white wine, then sprinkled liberally with freshly-ground black pepper. The *Cozze ripiene* are mussels on the half-shell with garlic, parsley, and bread crumbs, and browned under the broiler. Among other mollusks in the shell, the smaller clams (of which there exist many varieties) are used mainly for topping pasta first courses, while capesante (scallops) and tartufi di mare (Venus clams) are generally used to prepare delicate antipastos.

5-*Orata al forno* **S** A gilthead (usually 2 to 4 portions) baked whole with garlic, parsley, oil, and lemon (or other ingredients) and sometimes served on a bed of potatoes and onions. Other fish that lend themselves well to baking or grilling whole are branzino, spigola (kinds of sea bass), and the various sea breams like dentice (dentex), mormora (striped bream), pagello (Pandora fish), parago (sargo or red bream), and sarago (white bream). Fresh-caught deep-sea fish is obviously more expensive than frozen or fish raised on fish farms.

6-*Polpo alla Luciana* **S** Boiled octopus served with a dressing of olive oil, garlic, parsley, and lemon juice. Polpo in galera is cooked in a hermetically-sealed pot with garlic, oil, vino, tomato, parsley, and hot red pepper.

7-Seppie in zimino S-P Cuttlefish casseroled with greens, garlic, tomato, hot red pepper, wine, and olive oil. Other foods prepared in this manner include calamari squid, baccalà, and lampredotto.

185

UOVA (Egg dishes)

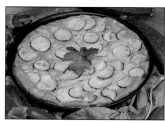

1-Frittata di zucchine M Omelette with zucchini rounds sautéed in olive oil. Squash-flower and onion omelettes are also delicious.

2-Tortino di carciofi M A puffy oven-baked omelette with sliced artichokes sautéed in olive oil.

3-Uova al pomodoro* S Fried eggs (not scrambled) with ripe tomato, basil, and olive oil (June – September).

VERDURE E CONTORNI
(Vegetables and Side Dishes)

1-Asparagi alla fiorentina* M Buttered asparagus with parmi-giano and fried eggs (April – June). Fried eggs may also be served over buttered spinach, in much the same manner.

2-Cappelle alla griglia* M-S Grilled porcini mushroom caps with garlic and parsley (June – October).

3-Fagioli sgranati* (or Fagioli all'olio) **M** White cannellini beans (or other varieties, including piattellini e zolfini) boiled with garlic and sage. Served drizzled with extra-virgin olive oil. **Fagioli nel fiasco** are cooked in a wine flask (with the straw removed) in hot ashes. Fresh beans are available from May to August. In other months, dried beans are the norm. **Fagioli all'uccelletto** S boiled white beans (see above) reheated with garlic, tomato, sage, and olive oil. **Ceci all'olio** M Dried chickpeas, soaked overnight and boiled with garlic and rosemary. Served drizzled with extra-virgin olive oil.

4-Fagiolini in umido* **S** Green beans stewed with onion, carrot, tomato, and olive oil. Boiled green beans are also often served with butter or topped with a garlic, parsley, and oil dressing (June – September).

5-Piselli alla fiorentina* **S** Peas stewed with fresh garlic, bacon (or prosciutto), parsley, and olive oil (May – June).

6- Verdure miste fritte, S: un insieme di verdure come **funghi** porcini (o d'altro tipo), **patate** tagliate a fette, **cipolle** a rondelle, **zucchine** a "bastoncino", **carciofi** a spicchio, foglie di **salvia** infarinate e fritte. I **Fiori fritti*** (fiori di zucca) invece, vengono fritti in pastella fatta con l'uovo.

DOLCI E DESSERT
(Sweets and Desserts)

1-Cantucci col vinsanto Dry almond biscuits, characteristically oblong in form, typical of Prato. Excellent dunked in vinsanto or similar dessert wines. Cantucci keep exceptionally well.

2-Crostata A flat pie made with short pastry topped with jam or fruit.

3-Frittelle di riso* Rice fritters: rice cooked in milk with egg, raisins, and liqueur or Marsala, formed into balls and deep-fried. Served dusted with granulated sugar (San Giuseppe, Father's Day).

4-Panna cotta A pudding made of cream, eggs, and lemon and vanilla flavoring - a richer variety of the so-called Lattaiolo (made with milk). Served with caramel or hot chocolate sauce or, in season, with forest fruits.

5-Sorbetto al limone Lemon sherbet: sugar syrup with lemon juice, crystallized (not frozen solid) in the freezer. Also made with tangerine or green apple juice or fine wines, liquors, etc. At the banquets of old, the sorbetto (today served at the end of a meal) was served between one and another course to "refresh" the palate.

6-_Tiramisù_ A trifle with lady fingers dipped in coffee (or various liquors) and mascarpone cheese; flavored with coffee beans and dusted with cocoa.

7-_Torta della nonna_ A short pastry shell with a filling of crème patissière, ricotta cheese, liqueur, almonds and pine nuts, and vanilla and lemon flavoring, dusted with confectioners' sugar

8-Zuccotto A frozen confection, typically dome-shaped, made with sponge cake dipped in vinsanto or liquor, whipped cream, cocoa, candid fruit, and grated chocolate. Served cold.

ALBERTI Leon Battista
(1404-1472)

Architect and Humanist. A multi-talented humanist, architect, treatise-writer, poet and author of dialogues in Latin and the vernacular, Alberti studied in Genoa, Padua and Bologna, and lived for a long time in Rome, although it is with Florence that his name is most closely linked. Here he distinguished himself as a skilled draughtsman and innovative user of perspective, knew and admired Brunelleschi, Masaccio and Donatello, glorified in the preamble of his celebrated treatise *Della Pittura*, and here particularly he conceived illustrious creations like Palazzo Rucellai, the facade of Santa Maria Novella, the tribùne of Santissima Annunziata, almost practical applications of the theories expounded in his most important and influential work, *De Re Aedificatoria*.

AMMANNATI Bartolomeo
(1511-1592)

Architect and Sculptor. After training as a sculptor at the school of Jacopo Sansovino, Ammannati began his career as an architect at the court of Julius II in Rome. Returning to Florence, for Cosimo I De' Medici he planned and carried out the enlargement of the original Palazzo Pitti, building the grandiose and solemn courtyard. This was followed by the Ponte Santa Trinita and the monumental Fountain of Neptune in Piazza Signoria, illustrious works that made him one of the most typical representatives of late Tusco-Roman Mannerism.

ANDREA DEL SARTO
(1486-1530)

Painter. Andrea Vannucci, more commonly known as Andrea del Sarto, was one of the leading exponents of the mature Florentine Renaissance, a true point of departure for Tuscan Mannerism which would later culminate in one of his pupils: Rosso Fiorentino. Among his works - in which covertly 15th-century forms are developed in a 16th-century style, and combining the sfumato of

Leonardo with the composed harmony of Raphael - we should mention the cycles of frescoes in the cloisters of Santissima Annunziata, the *Last Supper* of San Salvi and numerous, splendid paintings today housed in the Galleria degli Uffizi and Galleria Palatina.

ANDREA DI BONAIUTO
(recorded from 1343 to 1377)

Painter and Architect. The fame of Andrea Buonaiuti, or Andrea da Firenze, better known however as Andrea di Bonaiuto, is due above all to the cycle of frescoes he painted between 1365 and 1367 in the chapter-house of Santa Maria Novella, also called the Cappellone degli Spagnoli, a cycle representing a complex *Allegory of the Church Militant*. In those same years he also worked on a project for the design of Florence cathedral, which he reproduced faithfully in his Allegory. He worked in Pisa from 1377.

BEATO ANGELICO
(1400-1455)

Born in Vicchio del Mugello, Guidolino di Pietro became a Dominican monk with the name of Fra Giovanni da Fiesole around 1418, but went down in history for his exceptional pictorial skills as Beato ('the blessed') Angelico. His works, in which the search for pure luminous tones is combined with a figurative style clearly influenced by the models of Brunelleschi and Masaccio, still ennoble numerous rooms of the convent of San Marco, now a museum.

ARNOLFO DI CAMBIO
(1245-1302)

Born in Colle Val d'Elsa and trained in the school of Nicola Pisano, Arnolfo was a talented sculptor and architect. After having worked in Bologna and Siena he moved to Rome where he lived for many years. Here he perfected his art, succeeding in blending austere classical forms with the decorative motifs of Cosmatesque art, as numerous masterpieces testify. Returning to Florence in 1296, he distinguished himself as an architect, working on the most prestigious building projects: Santa Maria del Fiore, the Badia, Santa Croce and Palazzo Vecchio.

BOCCACCIO Giovanni
(1313-1375)

Writer. Boccaccio was born and died in Certaldo and lived a full and intense life marked by a great deal of travelling between Florence, Naples, Ravenna, Rome, the Tyrol and Avignon. An assiduous frequenter of courtly gatherings, he transferred and sublimated his own sentimental and literary experiences in a vast production of verse and prose. The *Filocolo*, the *Teseida*, the *Ninfale fiesolano* and *Ameto* are only some of the writer's most celebrated works, a prelude to his most substantial composition, the *Decameron*, a collection of short stories that with lively descriptions of great immediacy paint an amusing picture of 14th-century Florence.

BOTTICELLI Sandro
(1445-1510)
see page 65

BRONZINO
(1503-1572)

Painter. Agnolo Tori, more commonly known as Bronzino, formerly a pupil of Raffaellino Del Garba and Pontormo, was the official portraitist of Cosimo I De' Medici and a painter highly esteemed by the Florentine nobility. Not unaffected by the influence of Michelangelo, he developed a profoundly intellectual and Platonically abstract painting, as his portraits reveal, in which the figures, with clearly delineated outlines, look like motionless sculpted statues. The brilliance of the colours is also static, as if removed from every natural reality to turn to a higher intellectual life: we may recall for example the frescoes of Eleonora's Chapel in Palazzo Vecchio, but also the numerous portraits now at the Uffizi.

BRUNELLESCHI Filippo
(1377-1446)
See page 16

BUONTALENTI Bernardo
(1503-1572)

Architect and Sculptor. One of the most active and esteemed sculptors and architects of Florentine Mannerism, Buontalenti's name is associated mainly with the Casino di San Marco, the facade of Santa Trinita and Forte di Belvedere. He was also responsible for an elaborate design for the plan of the city of Livorno and the apparatuses for festivities and performances organized by the grand-ducal family, many drawings of which are now kept at the Uffizi.

CELLINI Benvenuto
(1500-1571)

Goldsmith and Sculptor. After training in the workshop of a Florentine goldsmith, Cellini was several times forced to leave the city after being involved in brawls and other violent episodes. He fled first of all to Siena, then to Rome, where he participated actively in the defence of Castel Sant'Angelo during the siege of 1527 and where he worked and was protected by Pope Clement VII and his successor Paul III, and subsequently moved to the court of Francis I in France. Returning to Florence in 1545, he was hired by Cosimo I De' Medici, to for whom he offered numerous examples of his excellent skill as a goldsmith and sculptor. For the Grand-duke he made, among other things, the elaborate and majestic statue of *Perseus*. In the final years of his life he demonstrated a certain literary talent, devoting himself between 1558 and 1566 to the writing of his autobiography.

CIMABUE
(1240-1302)

The work of Bencivieni di Pepo, or Benvenuto di Giuseppe, the Florentine painter known as Cimabue, was characterized by a balanced plasticism and intense passion that marked a breaking away from conventional Byzantine iconographies. Active in Rome in 1272, and in Arezzo and Assisi, where he frescoed the transept of the Upper Basilica, he later executed the absidal mosaic of Pisa cathedral before dedicating himself to the fabric of the cathedral of Santa Maria del Fiore in Florence.

COSIMO IL VECCHIO
(1389-1464)

The able and shrewd Cosimo the Elder was the maker of the fortunes of the Medici family. He exploited the inheritance left him by his father, a merchant, to acquire influence and power in the Florence of his time. Despite his position, Cosimo never strutted his power, and when he commissioned Michelozzo to build a new home for his family, Palazzo Medici, he instructed the architect that inside it should be a palace—but outside severe and austere. To Cosimo we also owe the villas of Careggi, of the Trebbio, and of Cafaggiolo, and the Church and Convent of San Marco. In recognition, the Florentine Republic honored his tomb with the legend *Pater Patriae*, "Father of the Country."

DANTE
(1265-1321)

Writer. Dante lived in a Florence ravaged by the feuds between the two Guelf factions, the Whites and the Blacks. Although belonging to the former, he showed substantial impartiality every time he was summoned to hold public offices, and yet finished by being overwhelmed by the conflicts. The exile he was condemned to inevitably undermined his sentimental attachment to Florence, where he would never again return. In spite of this, all his work as a poet and treatise-writer is linked to Florence, its significance so far-reaching that he is usually considered to be one of the founders of literature and of the Italian language: from the *Vita Nova* and the Rime to the composition of his eternal masterpiece, the *Divina Commedia*.

DELLA ROBBIA

A veritable dynasty of sculptors, the Della Robbia family - Luca (1400-1482), his nephew Andrea (1435-1525) and the latter's son Giovanni (1469-1529) - with their Florentine workshop were responsible for the production of characteristic ivory-white and light-blue enamelled terracotta. The expressive force and refined elegance of their works can be admired today in the Duomo, the Spedale degli Innocenti and in Santa Maria Novella, and betrays at times, especially in the case of Luca, the discernible influences of illustrious masters, particularly Ghiberti and Donatello.

DONATELLO
(1386-1466)

Donato di Niccolò Bardi, known as Donatello, was born and grew up in Florence, first as a workshop boy, then as an assistant of Ghiberti, and lastly as a close friend of Brunelleschi and Michelozzo. Summoned to work for the Opera del Duomo as early as 1408, he soon distinguished himself for the vigorous plasticism and the intense refined expressiveness of his sculptures. His work was requested to embellish the Duomo, the Campanile, Orsanmichele and San Lorenzo, and was greatly admired even outside Florence, in Rome and particularly in Padua, where the artist stayed for long periods.

DUCCIO DI BUONINSEGNA
(1255-1319)

Little is known for certain about the formation and activity of this Sienese painter, who probably grew up in his home town but certainly also knew Cimabue: lively new interests ensued which were grafted onto an early Byzantine foundation. Many works are attributed to him, all of a religious nature, though one in particular ennobles his name: the splendid painting of the *Maestà*, executed between 1308 and 1311 for the high altar of Siena cathedral.

GHIBERTI Lorenzo
(1378-1455)

Florentine, sculptor of reliefs par excellence, architect, painter, skilled goldsmith and author of the unfinished but highly esteemed Commentaries, Ghiberti came to the fore when he won the competition held in 1401 for the second door of the Baptistery. He worked on the twenty-eight panels for two decades, a period in which he also produced other fine works for the Duomo and the church of Orsanmichele. In 1425, again for the Baptistery, he started what would become for its spectacular effects and preciosity of style his masterpiece, the famous Gate of Paradise.

GHIRLANDAIO Domenico
(1449-1494)

Domenico Bigordi, known as Ghirlandaio, was born in Florence and although being apprenticed as a painter in the workshop of Verrocchio was inspired in his youth by Domenico Veneziano and Alessio Baldovinetti. But when in 1481 he participated in the decoration of the Sistine Chapel he displayed what would later become the particular characteristics of his art: a vivid realism, a clear descriptive tendency and the presence in his frescoes of celebrated contemporary figures, characteristics which reappeared in the great Florentine cycles of Santa Maria Novella and Santa Trinita and made him one of the most celebrated and admired painters of his time.

GIAMBOLOGNA
(1529-1608)

Sculptor. A sculptor of Flemish origin, Jean de Boulogne came to Italy in 1550 and, after a stay in Rome studying classical sculptures and the works of Michelangelo, settled in Florence where his services were hired by the Medici family. His output was extremely varied: from the equestrian monuments of the Grand-dukes to elaborate fountains, including that of Neptune in Bologna, a grandiose work in its overall composition as well as in the smallest details of dolphins, cherubs and mermaids surrounding the god, and sculptural decorations for the gardens of many Florentine villas and the Boboli Gardens which are notable for the splendid harmony between natural scenery and plastic form.

GIOTTO
(1267-1337)
see page 93

GOZZOLI Benozzo
(1420-1497)

Painter. First an assistant of Ghiberti and later a pupil in the workshop of Beato Angelico, the Florentine artist Benozzo Gozzoli was active in Rome and Orvieto before returning to Florence where he gave expression to a spontaneous and vivacious style often distinguished by a predilection for narrative, the small descriptive episode and naturalistic landscape. As a result he preferred large spaces on which to fresco cycles of stories, such as the extremely elaborate ones of San Francesco in Montefalco, in San Gimignano, in the Camposanto in Pisa and in the chapel of Palazzo Medici.

LEONARDO DA VINCI
(1452-1519)

Painter, Sculptor, Engineer, Writer and Scientist. Son of a notary, Leonardo left his native village of Vinci at the age of sixteen and moved to Florence where he attended the workshop of Verrocchio. Very soon his natural talent and thirst for knowledge took him beyond the confines of painting, in which he nevertheless proved himself to be the true champion of the revolution initiated by Masaccio. He moved from the Milan of the Sforza family to Mantua, and from Venice to Rome, with brief stays in Florence, and finally to the France of Louis XII and Francis I, where he died. He devoted himself to art, but also to mathematics, physics, biology, anatomy, and civil and hydraulic engineering, excelling as a sculptor, architect, scientist and writer; in short, he was the most ingenious and versatile personality of the Italian Renaissance.

LIPPI Filippino
(1457-1504)

Painter. Filippino, the son of Filippo Lippi, was born in Prato but trained in Florence under Botticelli, who strongly influenced his early paintings. Called to complete the Brancacci Chapel in the church of the Carmine and to decorate the Carafa Chapel in Santa Maria sopra Minerva in Rome, his art revealed a resolute search for architectural grandiosity tempered however by classical moderation and a constant veil of profound melancholy, to which were added, in his later works, clear references to the painting of Leonardo.

LIPPI Filippo
(1406-1469)

Painter. Filippo Lippi was born in Florence and when very young was able to follow the work of Masaccio and Masolino in the Brancacci Chapel of the Carmine, which left a strong impression on him. After working in Padua he returned to Florence where he devoted himself to an unending search for light effects, limpid colours and spatial depth, which initially brought him close to Beato Angelico though subsequently made him a precursor of Botticelli. As well as many paintings of a religious nature conserved in Florence and in Paris, noteworthy are the fresco cycles for the cathedrals of Prato and Spoleto, on whose execution he was working when he died.

LORENZO IL MAGNIFICO
(1449-1492)

The son of Cosimo il Vecchio and Lucrezia Tornabuoni, Lorenzo de' Medici was born in Florence and received a Humanistic education from childhood onward. At the death of his father, the seigneur of Florence, Lorenzo remained a private citizen but nevertheless concerned himself with the "care of the city and the state" and so became its incontrovertible lord. From that moment on his energies were directed toward consolidating and legitimizing his power; he exploited his incredible political and diplomatic abilities to strengthen his dominion over the city and indeed in all of Italy. Lorenzo was "Italy's weigh-scale" and made Florence the power that regulated the balance among the forces at work in Italy. The great mediator also reinforced his power within his own family, and even though his health became precarious as time went by he remained the enterprising animator of cultural life, and, as a typically "Renaissance man," he carried the city to artistic splendor, embellishing

and enriching it with the presence and the works of the greatest poets, philosophers, painters, sculptors, and architects of the time. Lorenzo himself was a prolific writer and poet; among his works are the *Canti Carnascialeschi (Carnival Songs)*, which include the noteworthy *Trionfo di Bacco e Arianna (Song of Bacchus)*.

MACHIAVELLI Niccolò
(1469-1527)

A man of extraordinary historical, political, and literary genius, Niccolò Machiavelli became Secretary of the second Chancellery of the Republic of Florence in 1498..From the time he completed his first diplomatic assignment, his dedication to this work (and to the relative reports he wrote in later years) was legendary. His diplomatic papers include *Del modo di trattare i popoli della Valdichiana ribellati (The Valdichiana Rebellions)* (1502); *Ritratto di cose di Francia (Affairs of France)* (1510); il *Ritratto delle cose della Magna (Affairs of Germany)* (1512). In 1512, after the Medici family had returned to Florence, Machiavelli was relieved of his duties and even suspected of complicity in the plots against the family; for this reason in 1513 he retired to his home at Sant'Andrea in Percussina, near San Casciano in Val di Pesa, where he wrote *The Prince* (his famous treatise expressing his theories on the skills and virtues of a head of state). Machiavelli's extraordinary capabilities did not stop at political theory: he was also a well-known literary figure and the author of such theater pieces as *La Mandragola* (1520) and *Clizia*, which dominated the Italian stages of his time and beyond—and he is also remembered as the author of the famous novella *Belfagor Arcidiavolo*.

MACCHIAIOLI (19th C.)
see page 153

MASACCIO
(1401-1428)

Painter. Little is known about the background and life of Tommaso di Ser Giovanni di Simone Guidi, born in San Giovanni Valdarno, and mystery also surrounds his sudden death in

Rome. Certainly he was, with Brunelleschi and Donatello, one of the protagonists of that artistic revolution that distinguished Florence in the early 15th century as a prelude to Humanism. He worked for a long time with Masolino da Panicale, who was also from Valdarno, and with him executed the frescoes of the Brancacci Chapel in the church of the Carmine, a fundamental reference-point for all later Renaissance painting.

MICHELANGELO
(1475-1564)
see page 131

MICHELOZZO
(1396-1472)

At a very early age Michelozzo worked in Florence as a sculptor, first with Ghiberti and later with Donatello, quickly revealing an austere and archaicizing style. But it was as an architect that he really established himself, displaying a balance and stylistic unity that was not extraneous from the influence of Brunelleschi. Such was his mastery that he soon became the official architect of the emerging Medici family, for whom he designed the majestic Palazzo Medici, rebuilt the convent of San Marco and worked at the villas of Careggi and Cafaggiolo.

MICHELUCCI Giovanni
(1891-1991)
see page 142

PAOLO UCCELLO
(1397-1475)

Paolo di Dono, better known as Paolo Uccello, was a much talked-about painter in his native Florence due to his introverted character and his critical attitude towards the contemporary Florentine school. Educated in the Gothic tradition and influenced by an important journey to Venice, he favoured the use of vivid colours and exaggerated perspective effects which were vaguely medieval and in certain instances even unreal, as can be seen in his Florentine works, in Santa Maria Novella and in the Duomo, in the frescoes for Prato Cathedral, and in the masterpiece of his maturity, the Battle of San Romano.

PARIGI
(16th-17th C.)

Family of Architects. A family of versatile architects highly esteemed by the Medici family and active in Florence between the 16th and 17th centuries. The head of the Parigi family was Alfonso, who died in Florence in 1590, the brother-in-law and pupil of Ammannati. Alfonso was responsible for the cloister of the convent of Santa Trinita, the first cloister of Santo Spirito, in collaboration with his son, numerous modifications of already existing buildings as well as the completion of the Uffizi. His son Giulio (1540-1635), the successor of Buontalenti as grand-ducal architect and director of court performances, was responsible for the enlargement of the Arcispedale di Santa Maria Nuova and above all that of the central body of Palazzo Pitti. His work was continued by his son Alfonso, who died in Florence in 1656.

POGGI Giuseppe
(1811-1901)

Architect. Architect and town-planner, who in his successful career with the Florentine nobility had demonstrated his skill in harmoniously combining English-style park and garden designs with the most traditional neo-Renaissance forms, Poggi was called upon to supervise the imposing urbanistic project for the systematic reorganization of Florence as the capital city of the united Italian kingdom (1864-70). He was in fact responsible for the demolition of the walls of the third circle of fortifications, which were replaced by a ring of carriageable avenues. This system then continued along the hills to the south of the Arno, where, with the opening of the celebrated panoramic Viale dei Colli, Poggi built his masterpiece, Piazzale Michelangelo.

POLIZIANO Agnolo
(1454-1494)

Poet. Agnolo Ambrogini, who took the name with which he went down in history from the Latin name of his native Montepulciano, was a poet, scholar and distinguished humanist, an extremely sensitive man who cherished a great love for scholarship and the beauty of art. A friend of Lorenzo il Magnifico, who gave him hospitality and entrusted him with the education of his children, frequenter and leading spirit of the most prominent cultural circles of his time, he composed verses in Latin and in the vernacular and was the author of numerous Latin versions of Greek classics. Leaving Florence in 1479, following the cooling of his relations with the Medici family, he travelled in northern Italy, where in 1480 in Mantua he composed Orfeo, perhaps his most celebrated work. Shortly afterwards he returned to Florence to assume the gratifying post of Professor of Latin and Greek rhetoric at Florence University.

ROSSO FIORENTINO
(1494-1540)

Painter. Giovanni Battista de' Rossi, better known as Rosso Fiorentino, received his artistic training in the school of Andrea del Sarto in Florence. However, he very soon revealed his tendency to go beyond the confines of Florentine culture, spurred on as he was by a troubled temperament that was reflected in the tormented forms and exaggerated chromatic tones of his art. After a stay in Rome, he moved to France where he became the official painter of Francis I. He was one of the inspirations of the School of Fontainebleau whose influence was felt not only on French but also European art.

SAVONAROLA
(1452-1428)

Born in Ferrara in 1452, Savonarola came to the important Florentine convent of San Marco as a lector in 1482, but was banished soon after for the intransigent views he expressed in the course of his sermons, in which, basing his reasoning on rigorous philosophical and theological principles, as well as the Holy Scriptures, he heavily criticized laymen and clergy alike for a moral conduct totally removed from any evangelical teaching. Returning to the city in 1490 and elected prior of the same convent, not only did he strive to turn San Marco into a centre of cultural and theological irradiation inspired by strict Christian observance,

but, following the expulsion of the Medici in 1494, he also fought for the establishment of a popular republic directly inspired by the precepts of the Gospel. Hated by the city's potentates, he was declared a heretic and burnt at the stake on 23 May 1498.

VASARI Giorgio
(1511-1574)

Architect and Writer. Born and raised in Arezzo, Vasari moved to Florence in 1504 to study in the workshop of Andrea del sarto and Baccio Bandinelli. A visit to Rome in the retinue of Cardinal Ippolito de' Medici enabled him to learn from classical art and architecture, and a journey to Venice brought him into contact with Titian and other Venetian masters, but this did not influence the typical Tusco-Roman Mannerism that became the main hallmark of his art. Returning to Rome, where he remained until 1553, protected by Cardinal Alessandro Farnese, he met Michelangelo, who influenced him in his choice of devoting himself exclusively to architecture. Summoned again to Florence by Cosimo I de' Medici, for him he supervised the decoration of Palazzo Vecchio and built the Uffizi and the Vasari Corridor. But among his most famous works an important mention must be made of his monumental writing, the Lives of the Artists, an exhaustive collection of biographies of the leading Italian artists of his time.

VERROCCHIO
(1430-1488)

Painter and Sculptor. The nickname by which Andrea di Cione is more commonly known recalls the goldsmith Giuliano Verrocchio, to whom he was apprenticed as a young man, but his fame has always been linked to his activity as a painter and above all as a sculptor who drew on the examples of great masters like Ghiberti, Filippo Lippi and Donatello. A protégé of the Medici family, who commissioned a large part of his production, in Florence he executed splendid works for Orsanmichele, the Baptistery and San Salvi, and in Venice the equestrian monument to Bartolomeo Colleoni in Campo Santi Giovanni e Paolo, which he worked on until his death in that city.

GENERAL INDEX

Art Notes

What to eat in Florence